Broad Street – Newark, New Jersey

The Gospel is good for the church, city hall, and the marketplace,
for on the street is the place for Sovereign grace.
~ William T. Iverson, NTC. ~

JESUS
AND THE
WAYS OF SOCRATES

HUMAN-SHAPED EDUCATION FOR THE
TWENTY-FIRST CENTURY

———————

DR. WILLIAM T. IVERSON

CROSSBOOKS
PUBLISHING

CrossBooks™
A Division of LifeWay
1663 Liberty Drive
Bloomington, IN 47403
www.crossbooks.com
Phone: 1-866-879-0502

First published by CrossBooks 11/19/2012

ISBN: 978-1-4627-2033-0 (sc)
ISBN: 978-1-4627-2035-4 (hc)
ISBN: 978-1-4627-2032-3 (e)

Library of Congress Control Number: 2012913702

Printed in the United States of America

This book is printed on acid-free paper.

This book is dedicated to Vivian Thorpe Iverson.

Vivian Thorpe Iverson
1893 - 1996

My mother was pretty, smart and feisty -- a redhead. On a June day in 1908, she spotted Dan, an innocent lad of eighteen, the best skater in the park. Her feminine wiles conspired to trip and trap the tall lad with her skates in a Savannah park. She captured the hapless creature known as the preacher. They were married for sixty-two years.

With one year of school to gain a teacher's certificate, she developed her skills at the three-room school on Tybee Island. As a pastor's wife she started a Sunday School in the old dance hall on the Tamiami Trail in 1927. It grew to twelve hundred children and adults with the unity and diversity of assembly and break-out classes; along with Bible, the curriculum included missions and memorization, exams and report cards. From her Junior department perhaps forty children went into the mission field and ministry. She led the Women of the Church with 250 women with twenty circles teaching them Bible, evangelism, mission, family life, and stewardship with accountability. Education started at home, a school where she taught the Iverson children to love language, history, music and the arts, and most came to know Christ at their mother's knee.

"Bibi" was an energetic and indefatigable visitor for both comfort and evangelism, putting the phlegmatic seat-worn pastors of today to shame. At ninety-nine when this picture was taken in her typical red hat and scarf, she wore me out visiting the "old folks" from Hollywood to Homestead, though she was often fifteen years older than most of her beloveds. She did push-ups and sit-ups until one hundred, writing three letters a day and reading three books a week. Her home was impeccable, her dinnertime a delight, and her conversation fun and edifying. Her five children loved her deeply and many hundreds and beyond rise up and call her blessed. She died at one hundred and three years of age in the strong embrace of her Savior, and her works do follow her.

They just don't make them like that anymore!

Bill Iverson

June 2011

Acknowledgements . . .
Otherwise Known as Gratitude

In Lilliput Gulliver discovered many strange things such as the political parties. The Big Endians cracked their eggs on the big end and the Little Endians on the small end. So much for majoring on the minors and minoring on the majors even in our fair republic. It was sad for Gulliver to see a diminutive Lilliputian headed for the gallows and to his utter surprise he discovered it was for the gross moral failure of ingratitude. The Rationale: "If someone was ungrateful to another who did something for him, then he would be dangerous to those who did nothing for him – *ergo* . . . such a person should not be allowed to live. " It would be impossible to acknowledge all those who have enriched my life and speak through me in this small book, but here is the short list:

My father, Rev. Daniel Iverson who imparted to me the wisdom of scripture and the art of asking questions; my mother, to whom this book is dedicated, who nourished my soul with the classics and the arts; my brother Dan, a Midway hero who regaled the suffering Marines on Guadalcanal with Kipling, Shakespeare, Tennyson, the Brownings, Poe and much more. His photographic memory took Professor Henry Lily to the foxholes, and I am indebted to both of them for my modicum of literary knowledge. I can still quote much that Danny taught me, and though boring to my grandchildren, I thank them for their indulgence; my brother Ned, whose great heart imparted me a passion and concern for all persons, made in the image of God; for my doctor sister Lalla, who gave books, great books, many books, and inspired me to write, though rather tardily; for Bill Brownson whom I met waiting in line ahead of me at Davidson College, and whom I still follow with a great and rewarding friendship—and he helped to love words.

As I wrote the book I thought often of Charles Dunahoo, who was elected as Coordinator for Christian Education for his growing denomination, a servant leader in an oftimes thankless course for several decades. Few it seems want to be educated against their will, especially nice religious folk. He is one of my great heroes.

How can I forget my wife, Sylvia, who had to re-read, and read again with infinite patience page upon page long gone and unneeded; for my friend Jose' Mojica whose fortitude is celebrated here for editing hour after hour, day after day with me, followed by my administrator Keisha Cole, and finally, the skillful Eileen Lass, who incredulously is the mother of eleven children, far beyond mere proofing being the best of tough editors; and as for my son Bill, he has encouraged me beyond words by not only reading my stuff but doing it—he can out-Socrates Socrates.

I salute my colleagues with deep gratitude who wrote insightful and practical essays that enrich this small volume—Dick Sanner, Mel Folkertsma, Richard Pensiero, and two shining ladies who still speak through this book, Ann Oliver Iverson and Dr. Norma Thompson, Chairman of the Religious Education Department, New York University.

In the realm of discipleship education, Robert Coleman, the principal contributor to this book, is *nonpareil,* He is a prolific author, having written hundreds of articles and twenty-one books. He is best known for *The Master Plan of Evangelism,* named in the top twenty-five Christian books in the twentieth century. Translations of his books are published in 109 languages, with English editions alone exceeding seven million copies. I thank him for being my brother, model, pastor, friend and inspiration. I read the *Master Plan* on my knees in 1965 and many times since. I have sought to follow its principles as a sacred trust. I celebrate his life in sending forth this book, having given over 500 copies of the book away to pastors and students in the last forty-five years.

Bill Iverson

TABLE OF CONTENTS

Foreword   xi
Preface   xiii

Part I: Histories of Socrates, Jesus, Cities and Churches, Education   **1**

    1:   Living the Great Commission: The Discipleship Model   3
    2:   Barefoot in Athens   19
    3:   The Art of Contrary Thinking: Maieutic Questioning   33
    4:   Sandals in Jerusalem   47
    5:   Tale of Two Cities: The City of God and the City of Man   61
    6:   Entropy: The Church from Birth to Death   69
    7:   Truth and Worldview   85
    8:   Biblical Anthropology and Human-Shaped Education: The Intellect and the Lecture   103
    9:   The Significance of the Arts and Humanities for Education   109

Part II: Incisive Insights – College of Fellows, ICSI   **115**

    10: Humanism and Inhumane Education   117
    11: Modeling and Mentoring – Richard Sanner Enhancing What Is Taught Through What Is Caught   123
    12: Tools of Education, Old and New   129

Part III: The Community: Where Facts and Formation Meet the Truth   **137**

    13: The Idea of a Study Center   139
    14: The Study Center as a Covenant Community   159
    15: Education and the City: A Modest Proposal   169

Appendix   177

FOREWORD

The practical question in education is not what is taught, but how to teach. This is true of any learning endeavor, but effectiveness in getting across the message becomes crucial when dealing with eternal issues of life and death in the Word of God. That the Gospel of Christ must be heard is clear, but how can it be communicated and understood by people whose very salvation is at stake?

This is the issue Bill Iverson addresses in these essays. Taking his cue from Socrates and Jesus, he postulates that the best way to educate is by teacher and pupil interacting together around the lesson, flesh on flesh, mind on mind. It might be called the relational model, or better still, an incarnational approach to education.

Bill Iverson is a master of the art. Having given pedagogy in teaching special attention in his Ph.D. study at New York University, he knows the field very well. More significant than his extensive academic training, however, is his personal experience. I have known Bill for many years, and can say that experiential teaching is his lifestyle. As a pastor, professor, school administrator, city missionary, street preacher, church planter, coach and father, he has ministered on this wavelength for more than fifty years.

I can learn much from such a man, and I expect others can, too. That is why it is a joy to commend this book to you.

Robert Coleman
Gordon-Conwell Theological Seminary

PREFACE

A Fresh Start in Theological Education
Shaping Pedagogy to Biblical Anthropology: Academic Discipleship

This book infers, implicates, and dictates discipleship – "obedience-oriented theology." We will visit the city and dying churches, humanism and pedagogy, tutorials, virtual education, and modest principles. One of the most compendious descriptions of theological education is found in Ezra 7:10, where Ezra **studied the law of God, practiced it**, and then **taught it**. In the preparation of men and women to serve in ministry, what is more necessary than this? . . . That they fill their minds with the Truth, and then make it incarnate in their daily lives, thus earning the right to speak that truth. The life of the teacher and preacher should be a foundation on which he can create a platform from which to speak to his contemporaries anytime, anywhere, in places sacred and profane.

Perhaps the most cogent description in a brief writing of how to teach the truth of God is found in Luke 24. The risen Lord used a discipleship and small group approach. He met with two and then a group of around fourteen people. He walked and talked and asked questions. He was the intense listener. He was ironic, acting as though he did not want to stay and eat with his friends. He modeled the simple act of a blessing. He taught that the Scriptures were inerrant, and based on them both His person and the work of redemption in dying and rising again. He had two table talks that were intimate and informative, as well as inspirational—"did not our hearts burn within us?" There was demonstration, encouragement, exhortation, instruction, and promise. There was vision and a plan, something to live for and something to die for. In all, it was the highest level of andragogy.

Pedagogy is teaching method and its principles, which with children often have diversity, but sadly, with adults is generally confined to the lecture. To use Margaret Mead's terms, it is vertical transmission rather than lateral transmission. Kierkegaard said that the lecture pedagogy was the poorest, and educational researchers inform us that it is the least effective method.

Let us adopt the term, andragogy using (Gr. *andros*, "man") instead of pedagogy("leading children"). This is teaching women as women, and men as men, not as mere children. The person is not a *tabula rasa* with blanks to fill in, but a person with information that may be used for him or against him. It is that dialogical endeavor that turns facts into knowledge which is truly possessed by the learner. If this knowledge is essential or existential Truth, it may *possess* the learner. This necessitates security, identity, and integrity on the part of the teacher; it allows him to risk the dialogue and to seek to find the other person as he is.

Matthew Arnold contrasted Socrates' manner of communication with that of Pericles, the golden-tongued orator. The latter was, perhaps, the greatest speaker in history, but his admiring auditors went away, forgetting what he said. With Socrates, however, "the point would stick fast in the mind and one cannot get rid of it." Research demonstrates that the overuse of the lecture method creates "passive acceptors of the opinions of others" rather than active thinkers in their own right. T. F. Stovall shows that learning recall and application are significantly higher in discussion as compared to the lecture method. True dialogue is not the pooling of ignorance, but a community of minds sharing what each has to offer with mutual corroboration leading to more truth.

John Comenius, the father of historic Reformation education, said it this way:

> *To ask many questions, to retain the answers,*
> *And to teach what one retains to others;*
> *These enable the student to surpass his master.*

What we are discussing here is the Socratic or maieutic (Gr. *maieutikos*, lit. "of midwifery") method. It is the process of eliciting from the other person what he thinks and who he is, that he may know what he knows and who he is. It also vacates false ideas and creates more space for learning content. It is education, which from the Latin literally means "leading out from." It is a more perspicuous view of education which consists in the drawing out of what is in the pupil rather than cramming into him a mass of material from without. It is very probable that our youth today are not being as truly and well educated as were the youth in the schools of Socrates, Plato, and Aristotle.

It is only in this human approach to education that there is a moral, ethical and spiritual dimension. It is here that character is built. Lamentably, much education in Bible Schools, seminaries, parochial schools, Sunday Schools and churches falls far short of this purpose. Why do we stuff heads with holy content, which never gets to the heart, while real truth puts on flesh and walks out into the streets?

We see in Jesus the Hebrew model of a loving God, which is none other than expressing love through teaching— while walking, talking, eating, rising and retiring, in the marketplace and by the gate. The dialogue goes on informally. School is never out, for it is in all of life, at all times and places, sacred and profane, at the dinner table or conference table, in a planned peripatetic experience in the city, or a walk, arm in arm, on a lovely river trail. It may include the exacting dialectic, adducing knowledge, or a maieutic experience, giving birth to self-knowledge. It is the early Greek model of Socrates rather than the scholastic model of the later Plato of the Academy and his student, Aristotle.

The question before us is, Can this be transferred into theological educational systems today, given the human element of inertia?

The answer is an emphatic "Yes!" Where there is the courage and creativity, and the desire to produce holy, bold pastor-teachers, missionaries, lay workers and Christian teachers. These live in the world in order to out-think, out-live, and out-die this generation. In the way of Socrates and detective Columbo, let me add one more little thing.

Out-reading This Generation

To out-think this generation, we will need to out-read it! To *out-Google* requires no real process nor does it facilitate the pause that refreshes (the mind). To *out-text* is to wallow in a shallow swamp of words. To *out-twitter* is simply to drown in a sea of three- and four-letters words and meaningless phrases signifying nothing. But let us talk about books and reading, and we will find the key to education.

In East Tennessee a poor lad named Paul Thompson got a second grade education. He lived in a shack with an old aunt with a library of two thousand books – – *The Harvard Classics,* and *The Great Books of the Western World,* to name a few. She read to him and he read all the books repeatedly. At thirty he went to a small college and passed a special entrance exam and graduated in 18 months. Later he received a Ph.D. from the University of Tennessee. Books!

It was Harvard historian Kenneth Latourette who said that the early Christians did "out-think, out-live, and out-die their generation." It is to our sorrow that we moderns know little of how to think, live, or die in that manner. Indeed, if we did, it would seem that there would be a concomitant effect. One part of the process of "out-thinking" should be found in books and study. There must be something to think with besides our brain . . . *ergo* nourishing a diligent application of book content.

This should be nailed to the church door in Luther style:

Needed: Wild Bibliophiles - Must be Voracious and Insatiate - Money and Experience Not Needed

Let me welcome you into the company of bookmen of the past who did so much with head and heart and hand. People like Francis Bacon and John Wesley could think because they wrote it down and they wrote it down because they could think—and by this they thought about us who would follow, that we might "read their minds."

John Wesley led a movement that was not born of mere enthusiasm, for it moved a generation for God and set in motion a salutary social revolution that is yet with us. It was a book movement and a reading revolution. He insisted that his helpers "steadily spend all morning in this employ, or at least five hours in the twenty-four." A young evangelist says, "But I have no taste for reading." Wesley answers with a "certain violence," as William Barclay points out, that the young man should "contract a taste for it or return to his trade."

Incidentally, Wesley wrote a mere 371 books(thirty with his brother) and many hymns. His reading was not just biblical material, but historical, political, medical, and humane. For every fruitful book one writes, he must read forty or more. He must be, in the historical sense, a Christian humanist. Whence come good grammar and the vocabulary that captures subtle nuances? And how may the imagination be developed but by books? The effect of television is the opposite, bringing deprivation to the right side of the brain (the imagination and creativity sector) as well as the left—where thinking should transpire. Yet Wesley was an activist, the world was his parish, and he rode over 80,000 miles and preached over 17,000 sermons.

Francis Bacon wrote in an essay that "studies serve for delight, for ornament, and for ability. The first is for solitude, the second is to beautify social intercourse, and the third is to bring sound judgment into the world for action . . . . For expert men can execute and perhaps judge of particulars one by one . . . [but] the plotting and marshaling of affairs comes from the learned." Thus the linear, one-dimensional man is not the learned man.

The secular "historical philosophers" such as Arnold Toynbee and the Francis Schaeffer types, religiously speaking, are generalists who give us perspective. Bacon warns us that "too much study is sloth," and that there are some who use study for escape or mere external ornamentation, with little application to life. There is the requirement of "getting into life."

As he further states: "They perfect nature, and are perfected by experience . . . studies by themselves do give forth directions much too large except they be bounded by experience." An application for the scholarly pastor is that he has a discipline to be among people in common life, in order that he might preach and teach incarnationally—in the flesh and blood of life.

Let none who take Jesus or Paul as examples of biblical thinkers deny themselves the privilege of a persistent peripatetic lifestyle. They wearily walked many a dusty road imparting their very being in word and deed.

Also from Bacon:

> "Crafty men condemn studies; simple men admire them; wise men use them."
> "Read to weigh and consider. Some books are to be tasted, others to be swallowed, and some few to be digested."
> "Reading makes a full man; conference (dialog) a ready man; and writing an exact man."

When Paul told Timothy to study, he was not talking about an arduous and unpalatable task. The Greek word means eager diligence, like an intrepid athlete ready for the race. To be approved of God is to avidly study the Word and study men, that we might "rightly apportion" the Word of Truth—meat for the mature, milk for the babies, honey for the unlovely. "Reading Christians," said Wesley, "are knowing Christians." He adds the cogent insight; "The work of grace would die out in one generation if the Methodists were not a reading people."

Read as though your life depended on it. Again from Bacon: "Histories make men wise, poets witty, mathematics subtle; natural philosophy deep; moral philosophy grave; logic and rhetoric able to contend . . .there is no impediment of wit, but may be wrought out by fit studies."

If you love God with your *mind,* make a study plan and do it now. In His light we see light, for He lights every man coming into the world. Daniel Iverson penned this prayer in 1926 and it was sung in one hundred languages at the first Billy Graham Congress on Evangelism in 1966.

May this be your prayer, dear reader:

> *Spirit of the living God, fall fresh on me.*
> *Spirit of the living God, fall fresh on me.*
> *Break me, melt me, mold me, fill me;*
> *Spirit of the living God, fall fresh on me.*

Daniel Iverson
Orlando, Florida, 1926

PART ONE

HISTORIES OF SOCRATES, JESUS, CITIES AND CHURCHES, EDUCATION

LIVING THE GREAT COMMISSION: THE DISCIPLESHIP MODEL
Robert Coleman, Ph.D.

This book is about discipleship because it is about education,
and Christian style.
"If we don't follow, we don't qualify. If we don't 'do theology'
we don't know it!"

Jesus calls us to be his disciples. The word means "learner," in the sense of an apprentice. By placing the emphasis here, he stresses not only their development in his character, but also their involvement in his mission to the world, an expectation finally articulated in his last commands to the church to "make disciples of all nations" (Matt. 28:19,20; cf. Mark 16:15; Luke 24:47,48; Acts 1:8; John 17:18; 20:4).

What may be overlooked, however, in setting forth the universal extent of his mission, Jesus specifies that the end result of all the activity—sending, going, preaching, baptizing, teaching and witnessing in the power of the Holy Spirit—are done, ultimately to "make disciples," not converts.[1]

Herein is the key to his plan for reaching the world. For disciples do not stop with conversion; they keep following Jesus, ever growing in his likeness, while learning the lifestyle of the Great Commission, and someday, through the process of multiplication, the Gospel will reach the ends of the earth.

To understand what this means, we must look closely at the way Jesus made disciples. His pattern of doing it becomes the interpretation of the command. Of course, some of his methods two thousand years ago probably would not be the same today. Methods are variable, conditioned by the time and situation. But principles inherent in his ministry are unchanging, and offer direction for his disciples in every generation. I propose to identify nine of the guidelines, all of which flow together.

Become a Servant

The place to start is with the incarnation, when Jesus *"made himself nothing, taking the very nature of a servant... he humbled himself and became obedient to death"* (Phil 2:7-8). That decision had been made before the worlds were made (Rev. 13:8), so the cross, having already been accepted in

---

[1] The Matthew version (28:19-20) especially brings this out, where the only verb in the passage translates "make disciples." "Go," "baptize," and "teach" are all participles which means that they derive their force from the leading verb, though the word "go" does stand in a coordinate relationship to the dominant verb. It could be translated, "as you go, make disciples." Though all the versions of the Great Commission declare the objective to reach the world and mention necessary ministry in accomplishing that end, only Matthew specifies the reason for all the activity.

advance, made each step that Christ took on earth a conscious acceptance of God's eternal purpose for his life.

Though such self-renunciation seems foolish to this world, it is the foundation upon which relevant discipleship rests, and the indispensable criteria for all fruitful ministry.[2]

In this chosen way of life, Jesus went about doing good, showing in works of compassion how God loved the world. People were drawn to him because they could see that he cared about them. Sometimes the crowds numbered into the thousands. Generally, too, the multitudes received his teaching with appreciation. They knew that he taught them as one who had authority (e.g., Mark 12:12; Matt 21:20; Luke 20:19).

The same holds true of people today. To reach them we must don the servant's mantle.

For a generation like ours that has lost its way, living by their feelings rather than faith, this may be the only way initially to get their attention.

How can you meet someone's need? Unassuming as it may be, this is how your witness becomes credible. Communication usually begins at the affection level. Don't you like to be with people who show their love? One who is known as a servant will never lack opportunities to make disciples. Soul-winners are first known as shepherds.

Building on this foundation, another principle must be recognized, one easily overlooked by persons especially adept at care giving.

Look for Disciples

Getting appreciation can be deceptive. The crowds shouted the praises of Jesus the last time he entered Jerusalem, but they did not understand who he was or why he had come. They wanted a Messiah who would use his mighty power to overthrow their enemies and satisfy their fleshly desires. Though respectful, they were nevertheless utterly self-serving in their interests.

---

[2]   The heartbeat of this principle runs through my book, The Master Plan of Evangelism, though it is not specifically listed as one of the principles for evangelism. I thought that it was so obvious that it did not need to be identified. Regrettably, what is obvious may not always be recognized. So now when I lecture on the Master's Plan of Evangelism, I start with this principle of servanthood. Someday if I ever rewrite the book, you will see it listed first.

Making the situation worse, the masses, like lost sheep, had no one to lead them in the things of God (Matt. 9:26). Oh, yes, there were those like the scribes and priests, who were supposed to give direction, but they were themselves blind to the truth (Matt. 15:14; Luke 6:39). Jesus was doing all he could to help them, but in the incarnation he assumed the limitation of a body and could not give attention to all the people needing help. Unless some co-workers could be raised up—redeemed men and women with hearts like that of a shepherd—there was no way the waiting harvest of souls could be gathered (Matt. 9:37, 38).

So while ministering to the multitudes, Jesus concentrated upon making some disciples who could learn to reproduce his life and mission. His first disciples were found largely within his home environment in Galilee. In culture, education, and religious orientation they had much in common. To be sure, they were not generally the most socially astute people, perhaps not even the most religious. None of them, for example, were from the Levitical priesthood. Yet Jesus saw in these untrained laypersons the potential for turning the world upside down. Though often superficial in their comprehension of spiritual reality, with the exception of the traitor, they were teachable. Such persons can be molded into a new image. This requires a long-term approach to reaching the world.

Too easily, we have been satisfied with short-lived efforts to see masses of people turn to Christ without assuring their discipleship. In so doing we have inadvertently added to the problem in evangelism rather than its solution.

Discipling is best accomplished with a few persons providently drawn into your life.[3] It is no accident. They are the answer to your prayers (Matt. 9:38).

---

[3] The concentration of Jesus upon a comparatively few disciples in no way belittles massive evangelistic efforts. In fact, crowds were attracted to Jesus' ministry, and if all the women and children had been counted along with the men (said to be about 5,000), I expect there were sometimes 25,000 people in attendance (Matt. 14:2 1; 15:38). We cannot forget, too, that some of Jesus' disciples came out of the large gatherings of John the Baptist. While discipling takes place largely in personal relationships, colossal evangelistic endeavors present opportunities to preach the Gospel to multitudes, and to call out people who want to follow Christ. Mass evangelism has always been a part of the ministry of the church, and will continue to be so. We can be grateful that the Spirit of God raises up persons who especially are gifted in this work.

Likely they are persons with whom you already have much in common, beginning with your family and reaching out from there to neighbors and friends. Within this natural sphere of influence you will have your greatest opportunity to change the world. Though you are not the only person impacting their life, for a period of time you may be one of the most significant influences in their Christian growth.

Build a Relationship

As the disciples grew, Jesus chose twelve to be "with him" in a special comradeship (Mark 3:14). Of course, he continued to relate to others as the fellowship of believers increased through his ministry, but it is apparent that he gave a diminishing priority of attention to those outside the apostolic company. Even within this select group, Peter, James and John enjoyed a closer relationship.

What is also impressive to me is the deliberate way in which Jesus proportioned his life to persons in training. It also illustrates a basic principle of teaching: the smaller the size of the group being taught, the greater the opportunity for learning. In a profound sense, he is showing us how the Great Commission can become the central purpose of every family circle, every small group gathering, and every close friendship in this life.

For the better part of three years, Jesus stayed with his pupils. They walked the highways and streets together; they sailed on the lake together; they visited friends together; they went to the synagogue and temple together; and they worked together. Have you noticed that Jesus seldom did anything alone? Imagine! He came to save the world—and finally, he dies on the cross for all humankind; yet while here he spends more time with a handful of disciples than everybody else in the world put together.

There is nothing new in this pattern, of course. He is simply incorporating in his lifestyle the dynamics of the family, the foundation for learning. It was God's plan in the beginning when he instituted marriage, and ordained that out of this relationship Adam and Eve could "be fruitful, multiply, fill the earth and subdue it"—the first glimpse of the Great Commission (Gen. 1:28).[4]

What God planned for the home, where everyone feels loved and needed, is still the best way to win the world. Making disciples is like raising kids, and the closer we get to this family style of education, the better our methods will be. Here, in this natural environment with parents, and perhaps even grandparents, and likely some brothers and sisters, our values are largely formed. Family influences are especially determinative in the impressionable years of early childhood, for good or ill.[5] That is why close personal relationships are crucial in discipling, particularly with new converts.

Like newborns in the physical world, beginning disciples need spiritual guidance to help them develop. You, as a more mature believer, can meet with them, answer their questions, encourage their witness, and make them feel a part of the family of God.

If overwhelmed, enlist others to help. In fact, much of this follow-up can be turned over to men and women you have discipled. Developing these mature leaders probably will increasingly occupy the larger portion of your ministry.

The more unpretentious the association the better, like having dinner or going shopping together, even having a round of golf. What a happy way to have some meaningful conversation! When everything is seen as a way of making disciples, nothing is insignificant; nothing is incidental; it's all part of the plan. Think of the excitement this puts into living!

Such casual activities, of course, do not take the place of formal church services. Both are needed, and serve the same purpose of making disciples. But learning comes most naturally in more relaxed family-like settings.

Some of this fellowship can be arranged in small group meetings, periods devoted to corporate times of teaching, Bible study, prayer and

---

[4] In terms of population growth, the mandate to fill the earth through multiplication has been fairly well realized, but in its application of discipling within the family, the spiritual dimension of the commission has been largely overlooked.

[5] Because everyone coming into the world is born into a family, all of us have the means to understand how disciples are made. So no one can be without excuse in fulfilling the Great Commission. Of course, persons raised in dysfunctional families have a disadvantage. The reality is, however, that no home is perfect, so all of us in one way or another have to learn from failures, especially our own.

anything else deemed important to the participants. In my own experience a meeting like this once a week has been one of the most rewarding disciplines of my life for many years. Find the way that best suits your schedule.

But for fellowship to accomplish its purpose, believers must practice what they learn. Hence, we see another principle in Christ's master strategy, so basic that it was specifically emphasized in the Great Commission.

Teach Learners to Obey

What facilitated the disciple's relationship with Christ, and made it so productive, was their willingness to obey him. Indeed, that is what made them disciples. He did not ask them to recite a creed, nor kneel at an altar; he simply said: "Follow me" (John 1:43, 46; Mark 2:14; Matt. 9:9; Luke 5:27; cf. John 18:19). Their obedience evidenced their faith in Christ.

This does not mean that the disciples quickly understood everything that their Lord said. Far from it; yet Jesus patiently endured their human failings because they were willing to walk in the truth they did understand.

Obedience to Christ, thus, was the very means by which those with him learned more truth. He did not ask them to follow what they did not know to be true, but no one could follow him without coming to learn what was true (John 7:17; 8:31,32).

Making the disciples want to obey was their love for Jesus. "If you love me," he said, "you will keep my commandments" (John 14:15; cf. 14:21-24; 15:10). Putting this in perspective, he added: "This is my commandment, that you love one another, as I have loved you" (John 15:12).

Absolute obedience to the will of God, of course, was the controlling principle in the Master's own life. Calvary was but the crowning climax of his commitment. The cross, having already been accepted in advance (Rev. 13:8; Acts 2:32), made each step Christ took on the earth a conscious realization of God's eternal purpose for his life.

Just as he found his blessedness in doing the Father's will, even so his followers would find theirs. From the standpoint of strategy, however, it was the only way that Jesus could mold their lives by his word. A father must teach his children to obey him if he expects them to be like him.

One might ask why there are so many professed Christians stunted in their growth and ineffectual in their witness. Is it not a general indifference to the commands of God? If we are to make any impact on this indulgent generation, the obedience of the cross must become more evident. Though post-moderns reject claims of theological certainty they are not blind to sacrificial love when they see it.

Is it not time that the expectations of the church are spelled out in terms of true Christian discipleship? If this seems too much to ask of the whole congregation, at least we can make it a requirement with those few learners God has brought into our lives, and like Jesus, instill into their faith the meaning of obedience.

To see this take form, disciples need to see in us a demonstration of what is expected. So another aspect of Jesus' strategy cannot be missed.

Show Them How to Do It

Following Christ, the disciples were always in school. His life was the object lesson of his teaching. By practicing before them what he wanted them to learn, they could see its relevance and application.

Take, for example, his habit of prayer. It was no accident that Jesus let his disciples observe the priority of this spiritual discipline. Inevitably the time came when they asked him, "Lord, teach us to pray" (Luke 11:1). Notice, in responding to their awakened desire to learn, he did not preach them a sermon or assign them a book to read; he gave them an example—the Lord's Prayer (Luke 11:2-4; Matt. 6:9-12).

In the same way Jesus taught his disciples the importance and use of Scripture, the meaning of worship, stewardship of time and talents, social responsibility, and every other aspect of his personal life. As to evangelism, it was so woven into his daily experience that it did not seem contrived or programmed, but a natural lifestyle.

Through it all, he was showing them how to make disciples. When finally he gave them the Great Commission, there was no confusion in their minds about its meaning. They had seen it lived out before their eyes.

Those of us seeking to disciple people can do no less. As Paul put it: "Follow my example as I follow the example of Christ" (I Cor. 11:1). We are the illustration of our teaching (Phil.3:17; I Thess. 2:7, 8; II Tim.1:13). Our disciples do those things they see and hear in us (Phil. 2:9).

Giving this kind of leadership puts us on the spot. Persons we let into the inner working of our lives will see our shortcomings and failures. But let them also see a readiness to confess our sins when we know the error of our ways. Our weaknesses need not impair discipling when there is transparent sincerity to follow Christ. In fact, seeing our imperfect humanness, others may more easily identify with our precepts. Furthermore, if we learn from our failures, abundant as they are, there is no end to the lessons we will derive.

Yet, more than a demonstration is needed. There comes a time for action. To disregard this responsibility can nullify all that has been learned, which brings another principle into play.

Involve Them in Ministry

Jesus was always preparing his disciples to carry on his work. So as they were able to assume some responsibility, he gave them things to do suited to their gifts and talents.

First, duties were small, modest tasks, like providing food and shelter for the group. Since Jesus was unmarried and had no house of his own, it was natural for him to graciously accept their hospitality (Mark 8:20; Mark 1:29; Luke 8:3). As far as I can find, our Lord never turned down an invitation to dinner. I was glad when I discovered that.

After a while he began to have his disciples more actively assist in his ministry—they were enlisted, for example, in baptizing persons who responded to his preaching (John 4:2). In another setting, he has them distributing food to hungry people that had come to hear him teach (Mark 6:30-44; 7:31-9:9; Matt. 14:13-26, 15:29-38; Luke 9:10-17; John 6:13).

The work assignments increased with their developing self-confidence and skill. Before long they were sent out to do much the same kind of work that Jesus was doing with them—healing, teaching and preaching the Gospel (Matt. 10:1-10; Mark 6:6-9; Luke 9:1-3; cf. 10:1-6).

Lest they forget the priority of training leadership, however, he stipulated that above the public ministry they were to search out "worldly" persons to spend time with wherever they went (Mark 10:11-15; Mark 6:10,11; Luke 9:4, 5). They could work across the community all day, but in the evening they were to return to the house of those people interested enough in their mission to offer hospitality. In effect, the disciples were instructed at the onset to build a relationship with a few promising disciples, and prepare them to follow up their ministry after they were gone. If no one could be found with a desire to learn of Christ, they were to shake the dust off their feet and move on to another village. We do not have the luxury of going through the motions of ministry when no one wants to be discipled.

Can you imagine what it would be like for a whole church to be involved in ministry? Everyone can do something. I am reminded of a riding stable in West Texas, which advertises that they have a horse to suit every taste. For fat people, they have fat horses; for skinny people, they have skinny horses; for fast people, they have fast horses; for slow people, they have slow horses. And for people that don't know how to ride at all, they have horses that have never been ridden before.

Well, I don't know what your taste is, but when it comes to the Lord's work, there is a horse you can ride. More to the point, there is a horse for every member of the body of Christ to ride. As a leader, it is your business to help a follower find the right horse. Certainly they can share their faith, though you may need to help them do it with greater ease and clarity. With your assistance, they can also get started in a discipling ministry with another person.

Many of the programs of the church also afford opportunities for service. Early assignments can be in areas where they are already prepared, perhaps helping in the nursery, driving a bus or working at a homeless shelter. As they grow in grace and knowledge, they may assume leadership roles in the Sunday school or the youth activities, perhaps eventually becoming deacons or elders of the congregation.

The beautiful thing is that whatever form ministry takes, be it structured or informal, whether in the church or in the marketplace, it fits into God's plan for making disciples. However, the fact that one starts out is no assurance that he or she will keep going. And there is much more to learn. Concern at this point brings out another step in Christ's strategy of evangelism.

Monitor Their Progress

Jesus would get back with his disciples after their attempt at ministry to find out what happened (Mark 6:30; Luke 9:10; 10:17). By checking on their assignments, asking questions, and responding to their queries, he was building in them a sense of accountability. They were also learning that to whom "much has been given, much will be demanded" (Luke 12:48). The experiences the disciples were having in their work became object lessons for Jesus to teach some new or deeper truth (e.g., Luke 9:37-43; 10:14-24; Matt. 15:37; 16:12; 17:14-20; Mark 8:10-21; 9:17-29). It was on-the-job training all the way.

Problems were dealt with when they came up. Though their progress was painfully slow, Jesus patiently kept them moving toward his world evangelization goal. He did not ask more from them than they were capable of giving, but he did expect their best, and this he expected to improve as they followed him.

To me, the most awesome aspect of Christ's supervision of his disciples comes out in his prayers. His high priestly prayer is the greatest example (John 17:1-26). Have you noticed how most of the prayer turns to these men "given" to him out of the world (John 17:6-19)? He prays for their protection from the evil one; he prays that they might have his joy in doing the will of God; and as they are sent into the world on a mission like his own, he prays that they will be sanctified to that end even as he sanctifies himself. Nothing must be allowed to distract them from the work to which they are called, for "through their word" the world will come to believe on him" (John 17:20ff).

Though he knows that in a few hours they will forsake him, even that his chief spokesman will openly deny him, yet his love will not let them go. He believes in them when they can scarcely believe in themselves. This is the test of a real shepherd. However weak and faltering his disciples may be, Jesus cherishes for them the highest that he knows in spiritual communion (John 17:21-26).

With this same concern, you, too, must lift up your disciple in prayer. Notwithstanding disappointments, keep before them the all-sufficient resources of divine grace. Frequently ask how they are getting along. Where fleshly traits are recognized, they must be brought to the cross. Rebuke will not be resented when offered in love if we build self-esteem in them through constant commendation of every evidence of progress in their developing priesthood.

Though we are perceived to be the leaders, let us make it clear that Christ is the authority. Keep the focus on him. Avoid any authoritarian role of a master guru.[6] Jesus alone commands. In subjection to him, discipler and disciples learn together. In this joint experience of growth, I have come to see that the Great Commission is the Lord's way to encourage the sanctification of his church. You cannot sincerely lead another person to learn more of Christ without being discipled yourself in the process. Remember, though, the ultimate goal is not our own piety but discipling

---

6   I have to take exception to some teaching about discipleship on a pyramid model, where a leader at the top issues commands which persons below must automatically obey. True leaders are not dictators, but servants. Like Jesus, they lead like shepherds.

"all nations" to the glory of God. This can only come to pass through multiplication.

Expect Disciples to Reproduce

Life inevitably reproduces its own kind. Careless persons who let the cares of this world choke the word of God will reap the folly of their ways. On the other hand, those living in conformity to Christ develop the qualities of his life and ministry.

His parable of the vine and the branches is a beautiful illustration (John 15:1-17). Jesus likens himself in this analogy to the vine and the disciples to the branches. The branches are conveyors of the life in the vine, and when properly functioning, produce a harvest. Any branch not fulfilling its purpose is cut off by the very watchful gardener. Even producing branches are pruned by the gardener in order that they may be more fruitful. "This is to my Father's glory," Jesus explained, "showing yourselves to be my disciples" (John 15:8).

When fruit bearing is seen in this larger context of producing Christlikeness—first in us and then in others—we find that practically everything Jesus did and said pointed to this truth. The Great Commission simply brings the principle into focus, phrasing it in terms of disciple-making.

The disciples were taught to live always with the harvest in view. "Open your eyes and look at the fields," he said, noticing the men coming to hear him in Sychar, "They are ripe for harvest" (John 4:35). The disciples could see what he meant, and could also appreciate its spiritual application, when he added, "Even now the reaper draws his wages, even now he harvests the crop for eternal life" (John 4:36). Whether disciples sowed or reaped, Jesus wanted them to realize that their work had impact on eternity, ultimately culminating in the gathering of the nations at the throne of God.

The key to the final harvest centers in the quality and supply of laborers obeying the mandate of Christ. It does not matter how few their numbers are in the beginning provided they reproduce, and teach their disciples to do the same. As simple as it may seem, this is the way his church will ultimately triumph. I know of no other plan.

Our Lord did not come in his incarnate body to evangelize the world; he came to make it possible for the world to be saved through his atoning blood. But on his way to Calvary, he made sure some of his followers were equipped by strategy and vision to gather the harvest. You can do the same. As persons close to you come to realize how they fit into this multiplication strategy, dream with them about their place in the harvest. It will be fun talking about how God will use their unique personalities and gifts in ways beyond your own. It's the kind of conversation parents have with their mature children before they leave home.

The time comes when they are so occupied in their own work that your relationship takes on a different quality. Though you are not there as before, a bond of love remains, perhaps even deepens. As these men and women move on, others will take their place, and the process begins again. With each succeeding spiritual generation, anticipation of the harvest grows, looking joyously to the day when finally disciples will be made of all nations, and there will be a reunion in the sky.

However, there remains yet one principle to understand, apart from which everything said to this point would prove insignificant.

Trust Them to the Holy Spirit

Having given the disciples his last command, Jesus said "Behold, I am with you always to the very end of the age"—the promise of the Great Commission.

He is referring to the ministry of the Holy Spirit. What God administers as the Father, and reveals as the Son, he accomplishes as the Third Person of the Holy Trinity. We are introduced to him in the first chapter of Genesis (1:2) as he creates the cosmos and later breathes life into the creature God has made in his image (Genesis 2:7). When persons turn to their own way, it is the Spirit who seeks to bring them back and effect reconciliation with God.

Throughout the Old Testament he can be seen at work making a people to be his witness in a fallen world (Isaiah 43:10; 44:8; 49:6). Though Israel fails her calling, a day is envisioned when one would come on whom the Spirit would rest without measure and who will reign over the nations (Isaiah 11:2; 42:1; cf. John 3:34).

Just as the prophets had said, in the fullness of time the Holy Spirit planted the seed of the Father in the womb of the virgin, so that she conceived and gave birth to the only begotten Son of God (Matthew 1:18,20; Luke 1:35). Thereafter, the Spirit directed Jesus during the days of his incarnate life. Everything he said and did was in the strength and demonstration of the Spirit of God (Luke 4:18,19).

Jesus taught that by the same mighty power persons who believe on him would partake of his life and ministry. He would guide them into truth (John 16:13); he would help them pray (John 14:12 13; 16:23, 24); he would give them utterances to speak (Matt. 10:19,20); he would enable them to do the very works of Christ, even "greater works than these" (John 14:12). Through it all, the Spirit would glorify the Son (John 16:14). That supremely is his ministry—to lift up Christ, and, as he is revealed, men and women are drawn to the Father.

It is not difficult to understand why Jesus told his disciples to tarry until they were empowered by the Spirit (Luke 24:49; Acts 1:8). How else could they ever make disciples who develop in his likeness? In their own wisdom and strength they were helpless. Only as Christ was with them—filling them with his presence—could they do his work.

We see how this begins to unfold at Pentecost (Acts 2:4). The witness of the church now becomes the acts of the Holy Spirit. Just as it was then, so the same is true today. It is the Spirit who incarnates Christ in us, reversing the self-centered value system of this world so that we begin to live as servants. It is he who draws out disciples, planting in their hearts the desire to learn. Our part is to respond to his initiative. The same Spirit forms the fellowship of believers, the church, even in our daily associations with one or two followers. Through his infusion of love our faith comes alive in obedience. By his indwelling we become a demonstration of what he teaches. The ever-present Counselor calls us to ministry and disperses gifts for service. He supervises our growth in grace—reproving, encouraging, enlightening, helping in prayer—always leading on to something better. Finally, it is the Spirit who brings forth the harvest. From beginning to end, making disciples is the work of Almighty God. We are merely the instruments through which he works.

Evangelizing the world in all its different forms depends upon the Spirit's possession of the sent ones. Just as those first disciples needed a heavenly endowment, so do we. The power from on high, by whatever name it is called, must be a reality in our lives, not as a distant memory, but as a present experience of the reigning Christ. Hindrances that obstruct his lordship must be confessed, and in complete dependence upon the Spirit of Christ, we must let him have his way in our lives. Though we can never contain all of him, he wants all of us—to love him and adore him with all that we are and hope to be.

The issue in discipling the nations centers finally in the enduring fruit of our labor. It does not matter so much how many we enlist for the cause, but how many become workers in the harvest. If we produce this lifestyle in a few, others will follow; if we do not develop this leadership, others have nothing worth following. Discipleship requires that we live in a state of spiritual mobilization. Reflecting this commitment is a simple lifestyle, unencumbered with the things this world seeks, that maximum energy can be given to God's mission. In the same spirit, material resources are held with an open hand, since they belong to Christ, and are his to use as he pleases in his work.

Whoever takes to heart the Great Commission will find that it demands daring faith, called fanaticism by the worldly-wise, but known as joyous freedom by the sons of God. Jesus is looking for such persons to follow him—disciples filled with the Spirit of Christ, burning with Calvary love, who set their course by the priorities of heaven. Christian education at its best seeks to equip these kinds of scholars. Call them fools if you will. But they know that in generations unborn their lives will still be bearing fruit in our ever-widening circle of disciple-makers to the ends of the earth and to the end of time.

NOTE by the author: *This chapter is the recurring theme in this book and all of my books, most* notably *The Master Plan of Evangelism* (1964, 1964, 1993), *The Master Plan of Discipleship* (1987), *The Mind of the Master* (1977, 1989, 2000), *The Great Commission Lifestyle* (1992); and *The Master's Way of Personal Evangelism* (1997). The same teaching also comes out in my books on church renewal: *Dry Bones Can Live Again*, (1969); *The Spark That Ignites* (1989), and *The Coming World Revival* (1995).

Read on as Bill Iverson now introduces the world's greatest disciplers, the pedagogical model and method for theological education in the highest Greek and Hebrew tradition.

CHAPTER 2

BAREFOOT IN ATHENS

Liberal education has free use of words and phrases rather than precision;
the opposite is pedantic . . . but do we perceive with (mere) eyes and ears, or
through them.
Socrates in *Theaetetus*

The question before us is an existential one. Do we need liberal education or mere training – something for eyes and ears, hand, computers and machines? Allan Bloom in his blockbuster, *The Closing of the American Mind* (1986) was bold enough to assert that what most college students need for the marketplace can be gotten in two years, and the rest of the university life is filler, having little, if any, educational value. Our visit to Athens brings us face to face with Socrates who is daily carrying on a program of liberal education, and any place was the marketplace of ideas. He is showing people what they do not know and need to know, and helping them to become who they are. He assists them to bring what is latent in the mind into clear consciousness, creating a process known as thinking. It included a moral dimension, as well.

Socrates used a dialectical process to elicit and clarify the ideas of the others, so that "incoherent apprehension" is transformed into "articulate comprehension." He is carrying on a purposeful discriminatory dialogue as a philosophic tool for midwifing ideas, so that a person can possess, explicitly, what was before implicit, buried somewhere in the mind. Karl Mannheim points out that thinking is not a solitary attainment, but a social one: "Strictly speaking, it is incorrect to say that the single individual thinks." The use of word-symbols for the thought process is a social heritage, a gift of many generations. All of our thoughts are in some sense born out of the thoughts of others. The maieutic way implies a *koinonia* of at least two persons seeking for a brain-child to be born.

Man is a bio-social being. He cannot escape time and space in his biological existence, nor his social existence which relates him to others. It takes two humans in time and space in a most intimate social relationship to bring a new being into the world. Education is that point in time and space where two minds meet. It is a magnificent thing that through classics one may meet a great mind that existed 2400 years ago. If one asks questions of the book, the Great Conversation is underway.

By classics we do not mean only books, but music and the arts. Who could deny that the contrapuntal conversation of Bach's music, or the *pathos* of Wagner's *Tristram and Isolde*, do not create profound thought for those who have hearts as well as ears to hear? What transpired in the soul's eye of Count Nicolas Von Zinzendorf as he beheld and sensed the passion of the *Ecce Homo* is a story of profound thought and transformation. It is tragic that so few young people in this generation have obtained sufficient content from the present or the past to which the philosophic questions may be asked and from which thought may be elicited. But one need not be discouraged. He may begin with youth as Socrates did, and take them from the vestibule of rudimentary thought into the vast reaches of the greatest gift bestowed on man – the cathedral of the soul. The arts and literature teach us, and particularly autobiography, that the soul of a human being may encounter the sacred Other.

Charmides: Philosophy for the Whole Person

Socrates said that he had to "stop talking or quit work," and moved his conversations to the street, much to the chagrin of his wife who wondered how they would eat. By doing so, as Cicero said, he "called philosophy from the heavens and established her in the cities of men."

It was in the *palestra* of Taurus that Socrates met with Critias, his young relative Charmides, and other friends. He reported the events of the battlefield, but they did not dwell on the war. Socrates turned the attention of the group to philosophy and inquiry regarding the state of the young. Plato has set the stage with these three characters for his first Dialogue.

Charmides was a handsome young man, even striking, and it was obvious that Socrates admired him. But his overriding passion was to behold the soul of the other. Perhaps at the same time he would learn something about himself. Socrates said that the lad could strip down and show himself to be a wonderful physical specimen, but "should we ask him to strip and show us his soul?" Socrates knew how to get to his soul, for Charmides was "at an age at which he will like to talk." The subject is not so much a topic, but a person to discover, and the quest has a spiritual nature as is seen soon enough.

Critias knew that Charmides had a headache, and he conspired with Socrates to make the lad think that the amiable philosopher and friend of the young had a cure for the ailment. It was an amusing scene, for there were several lads on a long bench, and when Charmides took the favored spot, they all moved down, and as Socrates noted, the last boy got bumped from his seat and "was rolled sideways."

Socrates asked Charmides if it was merely his head that was sick, or his whole body. Then by questions and accessions he gets the lad to see that his soul (the whole person) must be sick if the head is, " . . . for all good and evil, whether the body, or in the whole man, originates in the soul, and overflows from it." The discussion goes deeper. If the soul is more important than the body, then herbs and medicine are not the best cure for a person, but "fair words, and by them temperance is planted in the soul." Charmides has now agreed, inescapably, that man must be viewed holistically, body and soul.

Socrates and Critias complimented the admirable young man for his manner, and it led to the discussion of temperance. Socrates did not impose with a lecture on this subject which was a principal virtue in the Greek thought and ethos. He told Charmides that he would "share the inquiry" with him, but he would never press him. He would not use rhetoric or monologue which is a direct pressure, seeking to break a person open as by a hammer. Socratic dialogue is more like a wedge. If the first exploratory questions do not find an opening, a place to begin, there is not a beginning. The midwife does not induce labor and make the baby to be born before its time.

The cool communicator does not pick green apples. The patient fisherman will keep his hook in the water, hidden from the world, with the right lure for the right fish. The midwife's inquiry will not go beyond what the student will allow. Unlike direct communication, with each question and answer, the maieutic wedge may begin to open the soul. It will not break a person apart in the process, but rather put him back together, both with himself and with others. Sometimes he may even encounter the Ineffable Other, according to Martin Buber. Socrates was perhaps the first to do "contract" teaching. He procured a commitment from Charmides on his part to risk the inquiry, while Socrates promised, on his side of the bargain, not to go beyond what the learner would allow.

Socrates often opened up a dialogue by asking for a definition which admittedly could be a boring exercise in futility. But it is not so with Socrates. The definitions are not used as ultimate answers, as with technicians, but for humble beginnings, as tools in the maieutic process. He played tricks on people more than once with definitions. The Oxford Dictionary of English Usage is both an interesting and an eloquent testimony that the usage is the final arbiter of the meaning of the word. He begins by asking a question which the youth thought he would quickly dispose of with the obvious answer. "What is temperance?"

Charmides by now was quite forgetful of his headache. He answered immediately that temperance was "quietness." When questioned further if the temperate were noble and good, Charmides acknowledged readily that this was true. In what seemed at first to be going afield, Socrates asked about reading, writing, and running. It was discovered and agreed upon that swiftness could be noble, but did not have quietness. Now there is a contradiction, and alas the first definition is beginning to seem quite inadequate. By now Socrates had firmly established a pedagogical *eros* with Charmides. One would call it rapport, and more profoundly empathic understanding, to use the term of Carl Rogers. Rather than being broken by the failure, the relationship engendered courage to keep on learning. Socrates asked the young inquirer for another definition of temperance.

"Temperance is the same as modesty."

Now the two learners discovered together that temperance included the good as well as the noble. Often using Hesiod and Homer, he chose at this point to quote from the latter. Literature was appropriately employed by the Greeks to create conversation with the great minds and the strong hearts of the past.

"Modesty is not good for a needy man," quotes Socrates. If a man is facing a life and death situation, his modesty would work against his well-being. Now Charmides is faced with two contradictions. Temperance is always good, while modesty can be both bad and good. Therefore, they cannot be the same thing. A third synthesis develops as Charmides, perhaps prodded by the older Critias, volunteers a third definition. With ironic designs Socrates said something to this effect: "Shame on you, son, just giving me some second-hand stuff from Critias or some other philosopher." The lad is thus tempted to be apologetic, but the *eiron*, the ironic man, ended up making the assertion that truth is truth no matter who says it. Critias jumps to his feet. He wants to be involved. The maieutic artisan had now drawn the third party into the conversation, discussing the fact that temperance is "doing one's own business."

Many professional teachers are apparently confident, but such temerity endures only as long as there is the vertical transmission position – the desk, lectern, or pulpit safely intervening. The integrity of Socrates is observed here. The integral man is whole – literally it means he is untouchable or unblemished. His sense of identity is so established at the core of his being that he can get out of himself and into others. He is vulnerable. Socrates was secure enough to speak with philosophers and teenagers, according each the same firm discipline of "the search." He never ran from the dialogue, and always gave the others "psychic space" as Harry Overstreet called it. The ironic way of ignorance helped him to relax his colleagues as the dialogues progressed. Kipling expresses it aptly: "If you can talk with crowds and hold your virtue, or walk with kings, nor lose the common touch." That is the integral man or woman.

The direction of this dialogue becomes apparent as Socrates gains the accession that the knowledge of shoemaking, working with brass, wool, or wood has little to do with happiness. He finally led Critias himself to say that the knowledge of good and evil obtains happiness. The paradox is left open-ended. The good as found in the virtues under discussion are useless: "We spend all this time in definitions which end up mocking us, insolently proving the inutility of temperance or wisdom."

Then comes an ironic affirmation of Charmides that all the more hooks him for the Socratic inquiry:

> *"And Charmides, you are the living proof*
> *we are wrong . . . Let me advise you not*
> *to go by this dialogue. Regard me simply*
> *as a fool who is never able to reason out*
> *anything; and the more wise and temperate*
> *you are, the happier you will be."*

The conclusion of the dialogue is in keeping with the Socratic *ethos*, for the summary is that they did not find the answers. The love of learning rather than the precision of facts is cherished in Charmides. The youth felt his need of something more, acknowledging that he did not yet have the qualities of wisdom and temperance. The accessions of ignorance confessed by Socrates and midwifed from poor Critias produced this anomaly. The lad, instead of being discouraged, enrolled in the peripatetic school of Socrates. Charmides said that at least he knew one thing – he would follow Socrates.

An apt conclusion on the part of Critias is his commendation: "Very good, Charmides, if you do this, I shall have proof of your temperance." It was not a graduation, which says, so to speak, "School is over." It was a commencement that says, "I have just begun to learn." What was accomplished in this open-ended education which leaves some facts uncovered, some problems unresolved, and creates such deep anguish in the pedants and sophists?

It is this: Socrates did not so much impart some great corpus of knowledge as he did of himself – his unique person, his attitude, and his lifestyle. The maieutic way is a discipleship and mentoring manner which centers on the presence of a person, in a community of love and dialogue, transmitting the knowledge of the self. Temperance was never quite defined, but it was existentially demonstrated in the maieutic teacher.

Lysis: On Responsibility and Friendship

Dr. E. I. Rhone enjoys asking young people questions. In Shantou, China or Arendal, Norway, Mexico City or on the Lower East Side, he will accost the most unlikely prospect and ask: "What do you think of young people today in general? Is the world getting better or worse? Has life found a purpose? Have you found it?"

One stands amazed at the swift and enjoyable engagement of minds with existential and teleological questions put simply with sincere interest. But Rhone is surprised himself, that so many commentators in discussing the *Dialogues* neglect Lysis.

He says that "We need to get into the minds and hearts of our youth, and overcome, in some cases, vast alienation. The study of Lysis is the prism through which we see the refracted colors of effective communication with young people."

It may be nostalgia, some sentimental throwback on my youth, but I find the conversation of Socrates and Lysis of such intense and delightful interest, that I am somewhat captured and happily trapped in the mind of the youth. It is the second dialogue, and well placed after Charmides, for it moves from wisdom and temperance to responsibility and friendship. Actually it takes place years later, and we find an aged Socrates still an effective communicator. It is a lively and joyous time where the old man secures strong pedagogical bonds with a subject not too savory to adolescents – responsibility. But the topic of friendship is wisely included, a subject of high interest.

Certainly the generation gap has proved to be a chasm in many segments of society, and it would be well for parents and others who are involved with the formation of youth to understand these old, yet ever new, secrets.

The setting is an open place near the *Lyceum*. The characters are Socrates and two youths, Lysis and Menexenus. The simple questions asked the youths initially were, as in the approach of E. I. Rhone, through the establishment of rapport. Knowledge through further questioning would be precluded without a mutual social interest.

Which of you two is the elder?

In a few moments Socrates has the two boys laughing. They are at ease in the presence of the venerable and famous philosopher. He tells them that he will not ask which of them is the richer, "for you are friends, are you not? . . . and friends have all things in common." This kind of statement and the mutual accord gave them a warm feeling, a *koinonia* of persons necessary for true dialogue rather than mere words between three people.

Menexenus is called away to a religious service, something never obscured in Greek teaching, and the two who remain enter into earnest conversation. The conversation goes something like this:

"Do your parents love you?"
"Of course they do, Socrates."
"Well then, who drives the family chariot?"

Any reader will readily see that things have not changed. Kids are interested in driving the car – in this case perhaps a two-horse chariot. When the wealthy youth had to admit that he was not ready yet for it, and that a hired hand drove it, the truth began to emerge. Although his parents loved him, yet he had to develop responsibility, and it took time and maturity.

And as was further elicited dialectically, Lysis had to admit that a lowly slave was his tutor. Others bossed him, and he could not do what he wanted to do around the house. In other words, rich or not, although his parents loved him, he still had to empty the garbage. How familiar, and how appropriate!

Lysis was asked, "Did you ever behave ill to your own father and mother?" With the negative answer, Socrates ironically points out that those whom he says love him are preventing him from being happy by saying "No" to so many things. What a victory for the adult world (although the point was not mere winning) when the teenager came ineluctably to the confession, "The reason is, I am not of age." This is a dramatic and unforeseen moment for the lad. He may be forced to say the "R" word – responsibility.

The wise teacher-friend then moves to the positive, and they discuss all the things Lysis may do. The ultimate answer is found, and they discovered it together. It is knowledge, not age that makes the difference. One may trust his affairs to anyone who can handle them wisely. When Lysis acknowledged that he lacked the conceit of knowing much, he was in the Socratic School, for such humility is the "beginning of wisdom." Young people want to be loved and to appear wise and great. This confession was willingly given and was cathartic – a need for many such young people who have real guilt. Socrates demonstrates that not only youth are candidates for such a therapy, but also old soldiers and philosophers.

There is a calculated risk in this obstetric work, but Socrates was apparently successful. One would wonder whether such accessions would bring embarrassment, and the return of Menexenus would mean a cooling in the atmosphere. Not so! As his friend returned from the sacrifice, the philosopher himself comments:

> ". . . Lysis, in a childish and affectionate manner whispered in my ear, so that Menexenus could not hear, 'Socrates, please tell Menexenus what you have been telling me.'"
> The truth of the matter is that Socrates had told him very little.

And here is the heart of the maieutic approach, the *ex-ducere (to educate by leading out)* pedagogy that obstetrically helps ideas to be born into the broad daylight of the Truth. Lysis had been teaching himself and did not know it. What he felt was enjoyment and accomplishment – and a bit more maturity. The proof of learning was the interest in further communication, for the person and the ideas had become significant. In an off-handed way, Socrates indicated Lysis should tell Menexenus himself. This is precisely what the Latin couplet from Comenius called for – the three elements of asking, retaining the answers, and then giving them away to others.

The discussion on friendship followed the Socratic pattern of taking what seemed established, the obvious meaning of friendship, then disestablishing it. Next comes the point of humble admission, with a deepened desire evoked for seeking truth wherever it may be found. They saw that they were not friends merely because of definitions, because they had failed in that futile venture. They may not have fully known about friendship, but they knew they were friends. Therefore the *eiron* produced two more *eirons*. The existential fact of their friendship was the **truth**, and was greater than clever answers. Naturally, then, the teacher, even if imperfect, could be their friend also.

> *"Oh Menexenus and Lysis, how ridiculous that you two boys and I, an old man, who ventures to range myself with you, should imagine ourselves to be friends – this is what bystanders will go away and say – and as yet, we have not been able to discover what is a friend."*

The old man established himself as a friend of Lysis, who sought to tell another youth what had been taught him. Socrates had "taught" little but demanded much. The youths learned truth dialectically and personhood maieutically. Their pedagogical palates were all the more eager for exercise because, ironically, they were the medium of the message.

Laches (on Courage)

We will examine briefly this dialogue not in reference to the subject so much as to see the process – whereby true education ultimately touches the person. The situation of this dialogue is thus: Two generals are discussing the education of their sons with Socrates. He begins where they are, as usual. It is well to understand the whole person that one may experience the meaning of friendship and personality. But without courage, what would it all mean? It is in this dialogue that we observe the movement in maieutics toward what is known as *homologia*, summing up into one word that which the conversants own or confess together. Laches exults in the discussion, as he "learned" what he already knew: courage was not merely physical, but had moral qualities. He ventured to try the dialectic art himself.

An intellectual awakening took place in the two proud, elderly generals as they agreed with Socrates on their mutual ignorance. A therapeutic cleansing transpired, clearing out the mental cobwebs. The two generals agreed with reckless abandon: "Let others laugh, regardless of what may be said of us, but let us concern ourselves both with our own education and that of our youths, together." This was perhaps the founding of the PTA. The enlightened parents further agreed they should seek out the best teachers they could find for themselves, and for the two boys. General Lysimachus was so excited; he wanted school to start the next day. Those who were planning education for their sons with a certain teacher at a certain place discovered, much as in the Hebrew and Jesus model, that school was at all times and places, and for all ages.

It is encouraging that in the present generation there are so many opportunities for adult education, and that the Senior Citizens are front-runners in many cases, intellectually starved. Yet, there are many more who are stagnating, rocking away their later years, which medical science has extended beyond the three-score-and-ten. Plato is reminding us that it is not too late to learn, and to love it.

Nicias gives a rather long monologue, which shows that he had gained a clear insight into the cunning ignorance of Socrates, and for the purpose of comment, it is included here:

> *"You seem not to be aware that anyone who has an*
> *intellectual affinity to Socrates and enters into a*
> *conversation with him is liable to be drawn into an*
> *argument; whatever subject he may start, he will*
> *continually be round and round by him until at last he*
> *finds that he has to give account of both his present and*
> *past life; and when Socrates is entangled, he will not*
> *let him go until he has completely and thoroughly sifted*
> *him . . . To me, to be cross-to be examined by Socrates is*
> *neither unusual nor unpleasant; indeed, I knew all along*
> *that where Socrates was, the subject would soon pass from*
> *our sons to ourselves; and therefore I say for my part, I*
> *am quite willing to discourse with Socrates in his own*
> *manner."*

Plato's educational purposes are lucidly set forth here. Dialogical learning has intimacy and accountability, and thus, an honest dealing with the past and a forthright dealing with the present. It may hurt now, but the reproof of such cross-examination should be loved for its final end, which is the Good. It becomes a life endeavor – learning about oneself, and not merely one's son or some other thing, however important it may be. Paul Tournier said that the School of Socrates, to which he said he gladly belonged as a therapist, is one of the person, and helps one to discover who he really is.

One may make a distinction here. Strict dialectics are more objective, and may be seen as "persons discovering ideas." The maieutic dialogue is more subjective, and one might say it is "ideas discovering persons." And in the dialectic alchemy, one may end up a better person with better ideas.

Protagoras: Socrates and the University Professor

Protagoras is the university man, and his call is not "publish or perish" but "lecture or leave." He is a goodly man with many gifts, but alas, a commercial type, professional to the core. He lacks urbanity and humility, has little care for the blue-collar worker except politically, and is seldom wrong about anything.

A crucial element of maieutics is elevated in Protagoras. It is the necessity of the Socratic person to give his total person in a complete way to the other – who he is as well as what he says. The dialectic becomes sophisticated in this dialogue, as it is the fruit of the older Plato's pen. Although Protagoras is, perhaps, the mightiest Sophist of them all, and highly respected by Socrates, yet the usual elements of the dialogue as used with Charmides and Lysis are employed. But there is one element that has not been noted thus far. Rhetoric can be carried on with great excellence to a listening audience of "sticks, stones, and sleepers" as one wag put it, but maieutics is dependent on listening. The dialogue ends when listening does.

One cannot miss the insistent fact that Socrates listens with his whole being, with entire concentration. He even "hears with his eyes" the sly intrusion of Critias into the mind of Charmides. Socrates gives himself totally to the person and moves the conversation according to what he sees and hears. The effect of active listening is phenomenal. It causes those who are listened to, to listen. It quickens their concentration and whets their curiosity. It builds and maintains pedagogical *eros*, that mutual affection which begets a felicitous reciprocity of attentive listening. Such a relationship draws forth from the other person, as the rays of the sun from the sea, the distilled truth, which is there.

The model of the physical problem of the deaf and dumb is an apt one. Is it not a fact that someone who is dumb and cannot speak usually has but one problem? He cannot hear, therefore, he cannot speak. Out of the thousands of possible sounds, to say the right ones is impossible guesswork. Communication between parent and child, teacher and student, friend and enemy, requires above all things, listening. Socrates was able to communicate because of his respect for the person of others. The lively dialectic is forever sustained on what one writer called the "awesome power of the listening ear." The diversity of "personal language codes" learned by Socrates is a fruit of his listening. He communicates well with the tender Lysis, the pugnacious Menexenus, the austere generals, his biased judges, and the insecure sophisticates.

The Sophists may be seen in variegated forms and colors in these discussions; but it is to be noted that the effort of attention that Socrates gave Protagoras was the secret to the latter's dialectical defeat. He listened poorly compared to Socrates, whose faithful listening gave him the material to engineer a dialogical damnation to the proud but good man. Socrates earned a right to be tough with his opponent through his commitment and concentrated will to give full attention to the other person. Since the listening does grant respect, even where there is disagreement, often a mutual accord is preserved which allows the dialogue to continue in the future.

Humor with a Humanist

Protagoras was a humanist of the first order. Socrates is an actor of a higher order. When the arrogant Sophist knowingly stated the Greek "Humanist Manifesto" to the barefoot philosopher,

"Man is the measure of all things."

Here is what happened.

Socrates: "Oh, Protagoras, you are so brilliant, the greatest of philosophers. How can I answer you? Come on, Critias, let's go home."

Socrates begins to shuffle off, but hesitates, raises his arm, and says he has one more little question.*

"And what may that be, Socrates?" asks the arrogant pedant.

"Which man is the measure, Protagoras, you or me?"

Touché! The obvious strikes home. Man must have something, perhaps Someone, above and beyond himself to do the measuring.

Pure irony!

* Columbo's model was Dostoyevsky's Porphyry, who was modeled after Socrates, the novelist's hero.

Chapter 3

THE ART OF CONTRARY THINKING: MAIEUTIC QUESTIONING

_____

To ask many questions, to retain the answers, And to teach what one
retains to others:
These three enable the student to surpass his master.
From a Latin couplet, John Comenius

The concern of this book is existential – the problem of existence. If the survival of a society is dependent on its ability to educate, *i.e.*, to transmit the culture of one generation to the next, then it is incumbent upon each succeeding generation to make education its supreme task. Kierkegaard, Dewey, and Bloom have each pointed to Socrates as a teacher for his respective generation. It is time to listen and to gain the requisite skill for that desperate communication upon which survival depends. We are proposing that in the age of technology and cultural relativism, ways must be found to accomplish the mission, and that the maieutic enterprise is one of many helpful answers needed. Perhaps we can undertake a definition, not as Socrates would do it, but like Noah Webster: "Maieutic: "(lit. 'obstetric': used fig. by Socrates; to act as a midwife); pertaining to (intellectual) midwifery, i.e., to the Socratic process of assisting a person to bring out into clear consciousness conceptions latent in his mind."

It is in Book Three of the Dialogues of Plato that the mystery of Socrates' method is revealed. Socrates first coined the term maieutic in his conversation with Theaetetus. It comes out as a "secret" which he is "confidentially" telling his young friend, and for one interested, it is a good beginning point for studying the Socratic approach, its nature, and its use.

Theaetetus tells Socrates that he is troubled with his questions. Socrates comments that "these are the pangs of labor . . . you have something within you which you are bringing to birth." At this point Socrates did not boast of any particular femininity in his mother, but that he was the "son of a midwife, big and burly." His mother was a midwife of bodies, but he was a midwife of souls. He points out that a woman who never had a child cannot be a midwife. Three things flow from this. The midwife must be a person of experience (literally "from *feeling* around"), able to feel the pangs of the other, and yet maintain *ataraxy* (*Gr.* "without running"), a cool head; gratefully not having to have the child and thus be able to help in the birth. The midwife, says Socrates, is not a "procuress," getting the baby that is ordered, but takes whatever child (or brain-child), is born.

It is under this image that Plato reveals his epistemology – how to know what we know. Everyone has within him true and false opinions. What is in the mind, untested and untried in the created world of nature and men, is not knowledge, but merely opinion. How is it tested, as to being true or false? It is like this. One picks up a green apple with the opinion it is a Pippin apple, which is still green when it is ripe. It is possible that it is a big, unripened McIntosh. Opinion turns to knowledge in the sweet taste of it. Even if the opinion were false, and it is not a Pippin, the antithetical learning may be all for the good. The truly green green apple may lead a person to a good one.

This is why Karl Poppen admired Einstein for his empirical discipline, letting nature verify the theory that was first in his mind. If this is true epistemology, then maieutics may have a great service to render to this generation of multiplied opinions and so little knowing.

Socrates used an interesting analogy with Theaetetus. Some people are not "pregnant" with any ideas, so what can a midwife do? They need to be prepared. They need a "marriage" to another. Prodicus, a Sophist teacher, was suggested as a good mate for Theaetetus, so he could have "brain" children. By this we see that Socrates is not discounting the necessity of content, and that people indeed must think with more than their brains.

The art is wonderfully illustrated as Socrates engages his young friend in the discussion of becoming and being. He speaks of the Sophists who "know all that can be known about the mind, and argue only out of the superfluity of their wits." He then is inclusive of his student in saying with tongue in cheek:" But you and I, who have no professional aims, only desire to see the mutual relation of these principles, whether they are consistent with each other or quite irreconcilable."

We see the irony of the two approaches. The Sophist claims knowledge, the Socratic person disclaims it. The former claim leads to monologue, and the second to dialogue. One leads to the lecture hall, the other to the marketplace. The first says, "Listen to me, I know the facts," while the midwife of ideas says, "Let us discover the facts together and see how they relate to each other – mutual learnings for mutual learners."

Every one of us understands the feeling when the pedant, who will not pay the price of the Socratic quest, quotes Roberts Rules, the Bible, a cliché, an aphorism or his own experience as authoritative. It is out of a shallow knowing, a knowing of the facts but not the Truth. It is all too often merely a defense tactic. What could be more modern than this comment?

> . . . *as for the argument of questions, and*
> *quietly asking and answering in turn, they*
> *can no more do that than they can fly . . .*
> *If you ask any of them a question, he will*
> *produce, as from a quiver, sayings brief and*
> *dark, and shoot them at you; and if you in-*
> *quire the reason of what he has said, he will*
> *hit you with some new-fangled word.*

The maieutic enterprise calls for the commitment of the whole being, and therefore takes whole persons. Surely for this reason the Delphic Oracle instructs us as it did Socrates: "Know Thyself." Two thousand years later, young John Calvin opened his <u>Institutes</u> with that very same point. True religion is composed of two necessities: "the knowledge of ourselves and the knowledge of God." He adds that it is difficult to know which comes first. But where do we find such whole persons? Socrates would say that it's the kid next door – or at the nearest gymnasium, to use a Greek term for school. Perhaps having examined the most ironic of men, a walking question mark, let us now look at the nature of the question itself. This is at the heart of the Socratic conspiracy – "tricking people into the truth."

The Key to Knowledge: The Question

We now move from the general to the particular; we see the question as a basic element in the maieutic approach. It is always found in dialogue, discussion, and forms of indirect communication. Jerome Eckstein shows that dialogical questioning is the means of native intelligence moving toward the natural instinct in man to find answers, to discover first principles. Education may be considered terminal when that child-like wonder has been blunted in children, so that they no longer ask, "Why?" What if Isaac Newton had eaten the apple instead of using that three-letter word? Maybe we would just be discovering Edison in New Jersey.

As the goal is truth, then perhaps Descartes' methodic doubt is a necessity. Questions are used to arouse anxiety and doubt in the listener as to the state of his soul and his knowledge (Socrates). Such an anxiety or hunger begins and is sustained by questions in many forms, both explicit and implicit. As the maieutic teacher and counselor holds a high view of man, he seeks the "inner self" through questions, while he seeks to solve problems in a koinonia of mutual learning.

In the humbling of the fellow "seeker of truth" through hard questions, the maieutic teacher ultimately extracts a commitment to truth, as he reveals defects in the subject's knowledge. A common love of knowledge, a friendship in truth, is developed in the mutual inquiry. In Buber's view, an "awakening" follows which "leads to change, and demonstrates how the question is central in this." One might say that all questions lead to the Garden of Eden, not for utopic escape, but to answer the question, "Where art thou, Adam?" Martin Buber's philosophy of the I-Thou makes note of the Shepherd King David's response to his humble survey of the majestic universe, "What is man, that thou art mindful of him?" This question has been proper in every generation since the beginning of time.

Over two *millennia* later Thomas A' Kempis comments: "Better of a surety is a lowly peasant who serves God, than a proud philosopher who watcheth the heavens and neglecteth the knowledge of himself." We remember that when the two generals were considering whether to commit their sons to Socrates' teaching, they realized that ultimately that they would end up talking not about their sons, but about themselves. Although questioning brought out content, in the process it led to a birth of self-knowledge, and the *arche* (first principle) would stand either for them or against them. Watch out for that cunning little maieutic gnome worming his way into both heart and mind! And for you who would lead, "Take heed to thyself." Then care for the sheep. (Acts 20:28)

The Ethos and Elements of the Question

There is drama in the dialogue of the questioner. The dramatic aspect of the question is that it has a distant end, as does a play. Dewey said that the question must pervade all, and having awakened one, to maintain curiosity, which does "assume a definite intellectual character . . . whereas immediate asking and answering discharges curiosity." The technocrat, with full knowledge of the outcome, will watch a basketball game on video in a disabused manner. But a Celtics fan closes his ears to all information on scores for a game already played. Even that sinking feeling of ultimate loss to the Lakers cannot discharge the dramatic interest as to the final outcome. If the playwright told the end of the story at the beginning, there would be no *katharsis*, no sense of cleansing or relief, even if the end was tragic. We cannot claim that the Socratic communicator does not know where he is going, but the interest stays high for "he knows, but he will not tell."

The tantalizing question must forever be present in the educational process through the Socratic dialogue. The last page of Alan Bloom's mighty essay is a call to return to Socratic inquiry *in the university.* Why not in preschool and better still, as a lifestyle? Some years ago I was browsing in a used bookstore and found a rare book entitled *The Art of Contrary Thinking.* The thesis is rare in practice and is most relevant to this discussion: Without thesis and antithesis, questioning and raising an opposing idea against another, there would be no thought; without thought, man is merely a weak brute with a memory that promises more pain than pleasure. To understand light, there is darkness, to understand blackness, there is whiteness; good shows what evil is and, conversely, evil makes good all the more prized; abnormal psychology helps one to understand psychology proper. Chesterton saw thinking as finding comparisons and contrasts. Without this, all thought, particularly in the moral dimension, ceases.

> *I am he, and he is me;*
> *She is I and I am god,*
> *And god is me.*
> *He is my rock, my butterfly,*
> *And I am all and in all.*

Francis Wellman introduces his book *The Art of Cross Examination* by saying that ". . . the issue of a cause rarely depends upon a speech, and is seldom affected by it. But there is never a cause contested, the result of which is not mainly dependent upon the skill with which the advocate conducts his cross-examination." It is the contrary thinking that wins the day. Wellman shows how juries, especially in the large cities, are composed of practical business people, "accustomed to think for themselves, experienced in the ways of life, capable of forming opinions and nice distinctions, unmoved by the passions and prejudices to which court oratory is nearly always directed."

Matthew Arnold rightly observed that distinction when he said that Pericles was regarded as the greatest of speakers, but people would go away forgetting what he said. With Socrates, however, "the point would stick fast in the mind and one cannot get rid of it." Kierkegaard spoke of his day as an age, which, "knows, in fact, no other way of communication but the mediocre way of lecturing." He said that the lecturer of his day did not "exist in what he understands." The maieutic way allows for the question, seriousness and jest. Yet, it loves the lecture and a good book when these elements are made accessible to the learner. Plutarch described the ethos of Socrates aptly:

> *Socrates was surely a philosopher although he*
> *did not prepare lectures or mount a chair or*
> *observe a fixed hour for conferences or walks*
> *with his students, but joked with them, at times*
> *went with some to the army or spent time in*

*the marketplace, and was finally arrested and
drank poison. He was the first to show that
life at all times and in all parts, in all we
suffer and do, always admits philosophy.*

The Questioner

The questioner is a hero. Often he is the *third fool* (see Iverson, *The Third Fool*) brave and wiley. Read the history of the hero and you find a felicitous mixture of jest and boldness. The man of courage is a man of irrepressible humor and hope. He is looking for victory. He expects it. Hope is like a tiger, says Erich Fromm, relaxing under the sun by a gentle stream, and yet in a moment ready to seize his prey. The questioner is in an almost ruthless quest for the truth – an anomaly of civil humor coupled with a terrifying life-and-death commitment to the Truth and the hazardous journey to it. Socrates did not trust the serious man, for such was not sure of himself. If he cannot trust himself, why should such a one as Socrates? Find a humorless serious man, and you will find him ensconced in the safe place. He may administrate well and be excellent with facts, but he will not pay the price for the truth.

The maieutic teacher is secure enough to be open-ended, and can live with ambiguity and lack of finality. His goal is to make better people, humbler people, who in turn will love learning rather than the acquiring of mere data who in so doing learn nothing at all. It is, perhaps, a modern irony that our institutions insist on calling graduation commencement, which simply means the beginning. Critics of modern education perceive the conferral of degrees as too often more of a *terminus*. It may be an interment rather than the outset of an arduous, yet joyous, intellectual pilgrimage.

The maieutic educator, as revealed in Socrates, is a person of ignorance, naiveté, and humility. Of course, ignorance in this sense is not a vacuum. It is the humble admission that the knowledge that seems to be known is so tenuous and unsure, that one would make this trade-off: to be thought ignorant and arrive at the truth, rather than to be thought wise, and never arrive at all. A childlike question is more important than the approval of others. And a good teacher will take the outer question, the one that a student cannot quite form through lack of knowledge, and help him form the appropriate or inner question. A pedantic teacher will say that the outer question is stupid and absurd either by word or deed, and keep on pouring out unprocessed data.

This humility leads to urbanity, informality and a non-professional approach. It is Samuel Johnson drinking up truth with Boswell and company, having hilarious and yet deeply serious table talk. It is Luther, with his lute in a tavern, drinking beer and looking for hymn tunes. He is asking questions of the common man regarding the lyrics of folk ballads and what they mean. It is notable that Mendelssohn and Mozart used the tunes of the earthy reformer and transmuted them into symphonic wonders. This is humane, mundane, man-shaped knowledge discovered by *hominem socius*. "There is no learning without community," says E. I. Rhone in his unpublished papers. The *Symposium* is the framework of sublime Socratic teaching. It is the pinnacle of such informal learning. It is the best of educations at the best of tuitions – social engagement with eyes and ears and hearts—and a hearty appetite is in order as well. Only one had to drink hemlock with that meal.

This maieutic person is earthy, and at home in the world of men. The wisdom literature of Solomon talks of wisdom crying out on the street corner. Kierkegaard said that in antiquity and early Christianity true knowledge followed through "to live and learn on the street." Socrates was compelled by his insatiable curiosity to live his life in the parks and marketplaces of Athens: "I chose to fight for Athens at Potidaea and to walk the streets of Athens seeking the truth." It is interesting to note that only one of the Dialogues transpires out of the city as a proof of this sort of urbanity.

One must be careful not to overstate at this point, for we agree with John Henry Newman that the best of all possible worlds is the university in the city, with verdant paths and shady bowers; a sense of peace in the midst of action, and yet accessible to the Parliament, the business houses, and the centers for the arts where the best of learning may transpire. But the real place of quietness for that maieutic person, being formed and forming others into moral character, courage, and loyalty, is within; Truth, Beauty, and Goodness dwell there with Love, whether in the country or the city. Socratic ataraxy means literally "not to run," the quality of being imperturbable. Loving himself, he can love others enough to be gentle with them; secure in himself, he is able to risk misunderstanding enough to be relentless; liberated within, he is free at times to give the appearance of ruthlessness. Emerson sounded quite modern when he described this attitude as being "cool."

Education needs the confident open-mindedness described here for this present age. However, the modern men and women who desire to re-live the script of Socrates must be forewarned as Herbert Spiegelberg reminds us: "Those who seek the city of free discipline will be put to a solemn and symbolic death."

Paul Tillich supports Socratic inquiry when he says "man is free insofar as he is able to ask questions about the world he encounters, including himself." Those who go against the tide of a culture seem to have, through their self-knowledge, the freedom to ask the critical questions about life, values, and custom. Rollo May describes this person as one marked by "spontaneity, genuineness, originality and self-expression, which requires courage." Paul Tournier points out that man often runs from the dialogue "for fear of discovering and revealing his person as it really is . . . it involves both choice and risk . . . It lays one open to reply." In summary, the Socratic person who seeks to obey the Delphic Oracle, *Know thyself*, and acquires self-knowledge, is free to relate to the world of ideas, things, and especially persons.

The maieutic communicator is also one who has the sense of the unseen world. He looks beyond the soul to the Spirit, and the Absolute. If "higher education has failed today's students" it is because there is a paucity of philosophers of the Absolute to be found, even in a vast university. There is the Unknown, and perhaps it cannot be known, but the presupposition always made by Socrates and suggested by moderns such as the philosopher Allan Bloom is something like this: "There is Absolute Truth, the Good and the Evil, to be discovered in the physical and moral universe. It cannot be created by democratic process." As Erich Fromm points out, it takes courage to look for those certain values of ultimate concern, for pain and disappointment may well come. Solomon said, "he that increaseth knowledge increaseth sorrow."

Koinonia: The Maieutic Relationship

Language teaches us much about communication. The very word communicate is predicated on the *communis*, that which is commonly held between the speakers. *Koine* Greek is that which is commonly used. A *koinonia* group is a fellowship of hearts and a community of minds. The verb *koineo* means to communicate, to become a common partner in words. The partnership element in the relationship of teacher and pupil, counselor and counselee, parent and child, is crucial. It may be junior partners, but nonetheless partners, each having something to give and receive. Without it, what passes for communication is simply the transfer of content and may justly receive plaudits and good evaluations but it is the first third of education, omitting the *praxis* and critical thought (Socratics). However, such narrow pedagogy may be as one pundit put it: " . . . the transfer of the notes of the professor to those of the student without going through the brains of either." Today it would be "going from Google to paste with haste."

Does one teach data, concepts, or persons? If limited to data, certainly a machine would do for the most part, and books would suffice for the balance. But true education, formal or informal, calls for something more, something that has to do with *being* and *becoming*. It seeks to engender the *love* of learning, not merely learning. It is learning to learn as well as gaining information. The integration of knowledge rides hopefully on the integration of two or more persons, what we have termed the pedagogical *eros*.

How important really is this form of communication? Karl Jaspers centered much of his thought on the problem of communication, believing the future of mankind depended on its "effective solution." Fritz Kaufman's sympathetic essay on Jaspers said that in "a world inter-dependent as never before, the absolute will to communication . . . has become a question of life and death . . . the search for truth pushes toward a communication with others." Those others are not merely at a Summit Meeting. They are in kindergartens, in classrooms, and in families.

In observing family life, one sees that child development correlates with the family milieu. If there are good familial relationships, the upbringing of the child is advanced. Should not such a community continue to be the best matrix for learning? Erich Fromm saw that the process of teaching is important, for the main point is the development of persons, " . . . that kind of teaching that can only be given by the presence of a mature, loving person." A teacher with a good measure of content is incomplete; a science of information will not do. Wisdom is the truth personally appropriated by one *persona* and transmitted to another. Yet, it is never an empty persona, for it always has content.

Let me give a warning here to those who are looking for gimmicks, for the mere "how to's" of education. The maieutic method may be destructive when separated from the personal relationship. Through the inter-personal process, it is rather the maieutic *approach*, and not a technology of method. The angry, eristic hothead or the manipulative mind engineer could take some of these elements and use them for his agenda. But it is not the Socratic enterprise without koinonia-relationship. Herder warned that Socrates' "excellent method in the mouths of his best students could only too easily degenerate into mockeries and sophisms whenever the ironical questioner lacked the maieutic mind and heart." Love never fails. It is the safety net for true dialogue.

The process of knowing oneself transpires as one learns about the world of men and things; for some there is more, something apparently transcendent. It is a philosophical quest that must be known in the living of life. If Socrates' dictum is true, "The *unexamined* life is not worth living," the converse is equally valid: "The *unlived* life is not worth examining." Seeking truth and its consequences necessarily includes "harmony and conflict, joy and sadness" which are "secondary to the fundamental fact that two people experience themselves from the essence of their existence." And this, according to Erich Fromm, is made possible by love.

Educational history must concede that seeking knowledge is a social, not a solitary attainment. The very language used is a cultural and historic gift, shared by the many. It is arrogant pedantry that would claim otherwise. The Cooperative Learning Movement is a powerful educational program proving just this. It is not the mindless humanistic Deweyism, which seems to have as an end, cooperation itself. It is a human dynamic. Quite appropriately, the leaders of this educational movement are two professors, Johnson and Johnson, a team that has accomplished what they have, exponentially, because of their *koinonia*. If anyone could heal our schools, it would be J & J.

Jaspers, as an existential philosopher, is calling for community in his plea for "man to come to himself" as Western Civilization teeters on the edge of the abyss. This happens in a relationship when each becomes free. A man becomes free to be himself insofar as the other becomes free. Even Sartre said it like the proverb which speaks of the faces of two men sharpening each other as iron sharpens iron: "I cannot know myself immediately, but mediately; I seeing him, see me." Paul Tournier would conclude this strong support of community for learning in saying that when faulty relations exist between parent and child at the beginning of life, then future relations between teacher and child, the adolescent and the community, will be distorted.

Perhaps we are getting at the pervasive sickness of our society, which is alienation. Adler says that to the degree that a person has social relationships, given his own purposes, and moves toward them cooperatively, he is healthy. And speaking of health, Cushman of the University of North Carolina, in a classic study of Socrates, named his book appropriately *Therapeia* (1956, republished, 2010). He saw the dialogical way as salutary. It is either one's overt or covert agenda, which destroys others in "getting to the top" in a university, a church, a marriage, a nation, or a corporation. Let this be written on the heart:

> *The necessity to unite with other living beings . . .*
> *is an imperative need on which man's sanity depends.*
> *This need is behind all phenomena of human relations.*
> Erich Fromm, The Sane Society

In the proposals for human-shaped education for this century, we will define the dialogue and dialectic, and discuss the elements of listening, drama, humor, irony, and Socratic ignorance. It is enough to remember at this point that the maieutic communicator and teacher is forever the questioner, and in some sense, he or she should be a question. Socrates called himself an *eiron* (from Gr. *eirein*, to ask) – an ignorant man who is willing to ask. There is the ignorant man who ignores, which is intolerable. He is the agnostic. But there is the ignorant man who says, "I know very little, and although it is embarrassing, I would rather be thought foolish than not know. So let me ask just this one question." Such a man must be secure in himself with a sense of identity, while the lecturer, the person limited to vertical transmission, may be standing behind the desk to protect his fragile *persona*.

Irony is the dialectical or critical factor in the Socratic method. It is always found in drama and humor. Henri Bergson speaks of Socrates' purpose in irony as a way to "dispose of the opinions which have not undergone the test of reflection, to put them to shame, so to speak, by putting some contradiction to themselves." The ramparts of philosophy and all critical thought are the high walls of Truth against which the antithetical ideas may mount the attack. This is necessary for the destruction of the facade of truth.

True philosophy will not allow the moral or cultural relativist to vapidly insist, against the logic of natural law and common sense, that "A = Non-A!" The Question, the "Art of Contrary Thinking," precludes the nonsense of passing off linguistic analysis as philosophy; nor the irrationalism of existential theology as a science in the knowledge of God; nor a moribund educational system that excludes itself from the open marketplace of ideas. Certainly if we follow Socrates around in Athens, we will find that he lets none escape the question, not even himself. I can imagine Socrates walking through the halls of Hodge at Princeton looking for Postmodernism and sees it on a great plastic door. He opens it and nothing is there

CHAPTER 4

SANDALS IN JERUSALEM

And it came about after three days they found him in the temple, sitting in the midst of the teachers, both listening to them and asking them questions. And all who heard him were amazed at his understanding and his answers.
The Boy Jesus Coming of Age at Twelve, Luke's Gospel

S he paused outside the courtyard, wondering for a few moments whether it was another of her fantasies, and whether she should again risk rejection and abuse. She was voluptuous, taller than the average woman, with long flowing hair which blended with her dark robe. An observant person could yet see the form of beauty upon her hardened face. As she surveyed her present mission, the lines on her countenance began to soften. She swiftly took her bottle of fragrant oil and ran, unmindful that her towel fell from her right arm. Through an iron gate she went past surprised servants to a banquet table in an open courtyard.

It was the home of Simon, the Pharisee, a religious and good man; he was stiff and formal, while the honored guest was relaxed, obviously enjoying himself. To Simon, the guest seemed antithetical to himself in his bearing and demeanor. Each lived consistently with the names accorded them. *Phares* means separation, while Jesus was called Immanuel - God with us.

There are other vast contrasts in this dramatic scene: socially between the woman, Mary of Magdala, and Simon, the wealthy Pharisee; morally, between her and the person whom she approaches, almost as a worshiper of some deity. But he is identified as a Galilean, a carpenter's son and an itinerant preacher.

She removes the sandals of the Galilean, who seems to accept the affectionate overtures of this woman of an ancient and degrading profession. She is not a person of financial means, yet she extravagantly breaks the cask of exotic oil and anoints the feet of the Galilean. She is not the least self-conscious as she reaches for her towel, discovering it is not there. Her enthusiasm is even embarrassing as she takes her waist-long tresses of hair and begins to wipe his feet. Simon is astonished, and recoils at the social nightmare. The horrific feelings turn into repugnance toward the abject figure. His so-called "holy man" guest gives the obviously grateful and sincere woman only looks of approbation. It is love, not sensuous, but compassionate.

A dialogue begins as the Pharisee "spoke within himself" as Luke describes it. He found that his ideal image of a holy Rabbi did not fit with what was transpiring before his eyes. He thought that if this man were truly a prophet he would have nothing to do with such a person. Generalizing from this experience, and perhaps reading the reactive body language of Simon, Jesus addressed him, "I have something to tell you." With permission to go on, Jesus tells Simon something about himself, but indirectly, through a story.

There were two debtors. One owed 500 denarii, and the other owed 50 denarii. When they were unable to repay, the creditor graciously and completely forgave them both. Which of them will therefore love him the most?

Jesus did not seem apologetic about the forced choice confronting the religious Sophist. Trapped and wary, Simon guardedly answers:

"I *suppose* the one whom he forgave the most."
Jesus affirms his answer; the noose is tightened.
"You have judged correctly!"

From this point one might say Carl Rogers walked out and William Glasser walked in with his *Reality Therapy.* Whatever psychological relief Simon enjoyed from the honest admission was short-lived. The maieutic teacher became quite direct with both persons. To Simon he gave rebuke and to the woman affirmation and hope. Each of the characters had heard the message in the midwifery way, and learned that which was appropriate to each of them. Simon did not seem to know himself, and thus lived in ungrateful pride. It can be said of him as of all of us humankind, "You are worse than you think you are." The woman proves the paradox that "God's grace and mercy is beyond all one could ask or think!"

The woman humbly confessed who and what she was, and could go forth forgiven, to live gratefully as a whole person. She was told to go in *shalom*, in wholeness of body and soul. This narrative perhaps best shows how the maieutic way can be a two-edged sword, one side for defense and one for offense.

Another brief story includes the elements of irony through silence, paradox and surprise, the maieutic question, and direct communication. It is another dialogue in the care and defense of women. Again we find ourselves in a courtyard, not of a private residence, but in the temple area. The same polarities are evident: the Pharisees, who consider themselves holy; Jesus, who is considered holy by others; and a woman, who is not holy at all, caught in the very act of adultery. It was a contrived situation raised up on the platform of the unfortunate woman's act of infidelity. According to Jewish law, persons caught in the act of adultery could be executed with two or three valid witnesses. This is because the Jews believed that if the most intimate of contracts were not preserved stringently, honesty and truth would not be preserved in society at large. To these male chauvinistic prigs we ask, "Where is the man?" Levitical law is to be equal in justice and mercy.

The quandary of the trap was this: If Jesus did confirm the teaching of Moses, then it would be inconsistent with the perception of the common people regarding love and forgiveness as Jesus taught and lived it. Yet, if he did not condemn such an act, he would be found to be a usurper of the Torah, which every Jew was to uphold, and a friend to the adulterous act.

The atmosphere is electric as the confrontation is pressed. An ironic act relieved the pressure on Jesus and began to cause uneasiness in his avowed enemies. He simply wrote in the ground with his finger, remaining in silence. This is not the way of the usual leader, who is often so glib with ready answers. When Jesus did lift himself up to speak, he proposed an idea in a conditional statement, and then retreated into eloquent silence. "Whoever is without sin, let him begin stoning her."

It is as though he agreed and was saying that surely she should be stoned, but let it be done "decently and in order," in grand Presbyterian style. "I have a good plan. Let the best man lead us, the one with no sin, and then all of us can follow."

Dr. Paul Tournier points out in his psychoanalytic appraisal that the whole procedure brought out repressed guilt regarding the many women they had inwardly undressed and oppressed. One by one, from the eldest to the youngest, the *kategoroi* – those who put people in compartments to protect their own worldviews – slipped away. Luke, the observant physician, says, "Each was convicted by his own conscience."

The postlogue is a *denouement* of maieutic affirmation. The remaining actors in the drama are Jesus and the woman, surrounded by the common people, elated at the *coup de force*. The prosecutors are called into question as the defendant is interrogated.

"Where are your accusers? Is there none to condemn you?"
"No one, Sir."
The Judge discharges the case.
"Then neither do I condemn you. Go now, and leave
your life of sin."

Having been so nobly defended by irony, she is now affirmed by obvious questions, and exhorted to live a new and better life of fidelity. At the same time, the gracious warrior of that paradoxical encounter deferred his own unjust execution, but not for long.

These dialogues yield the qualities of urbanity, ataraxy, integrity, compassion and empathy in the maieutic teacher. They shine all the more conspicuously against the contrasting backdrop of the sophisticated and judgmental pedants. Employing irony, suspense, and surprise, and avoiding giving the answer when the true question was not asked, Jesus drove home a wedge, which opened the hearts of both the accused and accusing. The secure person is one who may best teach lasting moral values while exposing an amoral technology of facts and creeds. Such a charade of truth devaluates humanity into chattel slavery. Jesus of Nazareth was such a person, and his inner strength is all the more remarkable when one considers his life circumstances. He did not live out his ethic and religion *in vacuo*, and this caused him not a little trouble.

Jesus in His Situation

It is readily seen by these illustrations from the Gospel accounts that Jesus also practiced the humane and winsome didactics of Socrates. It was a different time and place, in a unique culture, yet there are striking parallels. Socrates dealt with human values moving toward the Absolute. Jesus assumed the Absolute, and dealt with human values. The age of Jesus had its religious Sophists known as Pharisees and Scribes. The latter were grammarian writers (Gr. *grammates*) who prided themselves in technical proficiency. Professionalism and commercialism were perhaps more blatant in Jerusalem than in Athens. Philosophy and education belonged in Greece to the aristocracy, while among the Jews, religion was everyone's business, but controlled by the elite.

The maieutic reactionist comes along to prick such vaunted balloons through a life of paradox and risk in words and actions. He is a man of courage with a core of self-knowledge and identity that few possess. The narratives of the Gospels of Matthew, Mark, Luke, and John have captivated the human race for some 2000 years. It is an historical phenomenon that these men, by and large obscure and unlettered, should create such an effect on the course of world history. The Gospels are scarcely the volume of a weekly tabloid, a mere fraction of the writings of Plato, yet they are a vast anomaly in the history of literature. Libraries, art museums, and concert halls, together with millions of churches, educational institutions, hospitals and countless societies conspire to give ample testimony to the irony of those four brief biographical sketches.

Jesus was a radical teacher, a more appropriate description than reactionary or revolutionary. How did he manage to get to the crux of things, in all of these life situations? He did so through bold irony and sagacious questions. He was a maieutic man.

The sovereignty of that day found its seat in Rome, and was administered through puppet kings in small kingdoms, mere pawns in the hand of Caesar. It was supreme Machiavellian pragmatism long before "The Prince" was written. These sycophants worked through the existing structures and institutions of their small governances. The people of the Jews, heirs of the now-hollow Davidic theocracy, were the unwilling collaborators with the *Pax Romana* and the *status quo.* The Jews had a rich heritage of oral traditions and written histories, dating back over 2000 years to Abraham. But there had been no "word from God" since the prophet Malachi 400 years before Christ. The culture was adrift and looking for the Messiah – an El Cyd setting his people free.

Many wars and conditions from the time of the exile to the birth of Christ had given rise to the synagogue and the sect of the Pharisees. The synagogue was an assembly of Jews gathered together to pray and to listen to the reading and exposition of the Holy Scriptures. By the first century, *anno domini,* synagogues were not only in Palestine, but across the known world, due to the *diaspora.* Along with its elaborate religious tradition, the synagogue was essential to preserving its people. The heritage and culture of the Jews had been propagated under subjugation for over 450 years, except for the glorious era of the Maccabees. Their religious fabric was woven from the various strands of Jewish life – Pharisees, scribes, Levites, Sadducees, and the Herodians. And there appeared to be no other *raison d'etre* beyond these except for the tax collectors and traitors who obsequiously served Rome.

The Pharisees sought distinction and praise by scrupulously observing external rites and forms of piety, while neglecting mercy. Jesus called them "whitewashed sepulchers," those who "cleansed the outside of the cup while leaving the inside unclean." That is why he told Nicodemus he had to be born with a new life from above, which was spiritual, not merely external. Having had no new revelations, the Pharisees took their "truth about the truth" and oral traditions and turned them into law. This gave rise to the scribes, learned in the Mosaic Law, sacred writings, interpretations, and language. The Pharisees believed in a personal God, the Scriptures as valid authority, angels, the resurrection, and other orthodox concepts as Jesus also did, yet they were his most bitter enemies. They numbered only six thousand, but their power far exceeded their numerical strength.

The Sadducees were the descendants of Zadok, David's faithful priest, and were the landed gentry with wealth and position. Although they were ultra-liberals, holding opposite beliefs from the Pharisees in almost everything, they "addicted themselves," as Josephus comments, "to the notions of the Pharisees, because the multitudes do not otherwise hear them." They were the humanists of the Jewish culture. Their blatant opportunism was seen in the secular worldview and lifestyle, which was occasionally traded in for the Pharisaic facade.

The antipodes are these: The Pharisees and Sadducees were separated from each other by their beliefs, super-natural and humanistic, and their way of life, pietistic and secular. Whereas the Pharisee was distinct from the common man by his uncommon religious performance, the Sadducee was separated by his riches. Jesus was a common carpenter, and "the common people heard him gladly." Both sects were in an opposite polarity to Jesus and to each other. The Pharisees especially were appalled at what appeared to be the ruthless iconoclastics of the "meek and mild" Jesus. He seemed to attack the Talmud, and was applauded for this by the Sadducees. These aristocratic secularists opposed his supernatural emphasis, whereas the Pharisees gave an approving nod to his teaching of metaphysics. However, neither group could deal with the authenticating signs he did, as the Gospels all record – not only miracles but love for poor, sinful and broken people.

As his teaching, preaching and healing became notorious among the populace, the Pharisees and Sadducees united in a solid front against the Galilean peasant in the third and final year of his brief teaching career. It was all the more embarrassing because, with little or no formal education and no credentials but himself, he spoke with an authority of which their second-hand religion knew nothing.

What form of teaching may a man or woman use which can be as a two-edged sword, both to carve a new heart in the common man, and at the same time, to cut out the old heart from the external religionist? It seems that in most respects, Jesus followed the same lines laid out by Socrates. It was so much so, that some have fancied he spent time in Greece, learning this pedagogy under Neo-Platonists. Consciously or unconsciously, he was maieutic in his total ethos, and he utilized the dialectic way to bring the sophisticates down to earth, and lift the earthly to heaven. The claim was that he created man and the universe and he seemed to prove that in his profound psychology.

Exegetical Studies of the Dialogues of Jesus

One writer in the seventeenth century noted that one of two divisions of Platonic discourse was the exegetic, and a subdivision was maieutic. Here we will seek to use the method of "opening out" the text to understand what is really going on in this indirect form of discourse.

The solitary experience of the boy Jesus indicates the early direction of his teaching style. Religious education was closely bound to the everyday life of the Jewish family. It was a sign of love for God that the Scriptures were taught in rising and retiring, walking and talking, eating and working, and even in conversation at the city gate (Deuteronomy 6:3-8). The devout family, as was that of Jesus, observed the three annual national feasts as commanded in the Torah. Faithful to their heritage, "as their *ethos* was," they took Jesus with a train of kinsmen and friends from Nazareth to Jerusalem for his thirteenth Passover – perhaps his bar-mitzvah. On the return trip, Jesus was not missed immediately, for it was a large crowd, and he was a reliable lad. Perhaps thirty or forty hours later, they found him where they had left him, in the temple. He was in one of the temple areas set aside for discussion, where even a lad could participate "as an Associate, a Joint-searcher after truth . . . . found out by mutual, amiable disquisition" as Matthew Henry put it.

They found him among the teachers, listening and asking questions. The Greek word used here carries with it the concept of careful attention, giving heed, and, in the religious context, with a sense of obedience. His attitude of loving God was to love with his strength by sitting at attention; with his heart by loving the things of God; and with his mind by asking good questions and giving good answers; and with his will, ready to obey the law.

The latter was certainly evident as he returned to Nazareth, having gained such notoriety among the doctors of the law. He remained subject to his parents, Luke records, for the law said, "Honor your father and your mother." There is no record in any Gospel about his activities until eighteen years later.

This model of teaching and learning as described here was not unfamiliar to the Hellenistic writer Luke. He readily perceived the early Greek (Socratic) as well as the Hebrew pedagogy in his narrative of Jesus' life. *First the boy listened, then he asked questions, then finally and appropriately, he gave answers.* As Mary approached, she asked him a mothering question, perhaps fittingly calling him aside: "Where in the world have you been? Your father and I have looked for you everywhere!" He answered her with two questions. He seemed secure enough not to make excuses or "protest too much." He simply packed up his scroll and quill and went home to live the life he talked about in the temple.

The Hebrew form of education as found in this scene is basically the small group discussion. Robert Coleman, in his book on the discipling model of Jesus (Chapter One), presents the thesis that the secret of the early Christian movement was through small groups. His brother, Lyman Coleman gave a lifetime to this aspect of Christian growth (see the *Serendipity Bible*). Mutual learning in a fellowship of intimacy and accountability was the basic strategy of Jesus in forming his *eklesia*. Since Coleman's book was published in the early sixties, it has become a modern classic for the Church Growth movement with millions of copies read in thirty languages. These small group principles are always present and primary where there is phenomenal growth in religious or even political bodies, as with the Communist. This is the way of "refounding the church from the underside," as Robert T. Henderson describes it in his book by the same name (2010).

Of course, the church within the church (*ecclesiolae in ecclesia*) was nothing new as evidenced by the *Unitas Fratrum* (United Brethren) who in deep piety reacted to Lutheran Scholasticism. Wesley also stayed within the Anglican Communion with his class meetings for the sake of maintaining unity in the Holy Spirit and Truth. As other religious educators have noted, dialogue and questions in a face-to-face manner are at the heart of the small group *schemata*.

Several seed ideas may be discovered here. The maieutic person is committed to heritage and history, as Socrates emphasized. He is secure enough in his identity to be at home with those of different age, education, and social class. He listens and interrogates, and does not tell all. He allows the conception to be locked in until the proper time. Mary did not understand, but she did "ponder these things in her heart." The young midwife of the heart was patient with the one who bore him. Luke notes, with a Grecian regard for the virtue of temperance and balance that the youngster "grew in wisdom and stature and in favor with God and man."

It will be sufficient and appropriate for the purpose of this chapter to analyze the last dialogues of Jesus, which, like those of Socrates, eventuated in martyrdom. The political and religious groups come with hard questions to find cause for destroying Jesus. As the drama heightens, the somber shadows of the Cross seem to pervade the demeanor of a knowing Jesus. Matthew brings all the sophistic forces together in one grand scene of deadly *elenchus* – dialogues unto death. The summary of these last conversations stands immediately before the trial of Jesus: "No one could say a word in reply, and from that day on, none dared to ask any questions." His enemies were left no options but to terminate the troublemaker. He beat them at their own game.

The baptism ministry of John was a point of great contention between the populace and the clergy. John was an odd figure in his camel's hair coat and rather unusual diet of locusts and wild honey. Many followed him to hear of the King and the Kingdom that was at hand. On one occasion he pointed to Jesus and said, "He is preferred before me because he existed before me." John was a relative, six months older. He was saying, in short, that Jesus was the Messiah, and that God had put skin on and personally visited his people. He even baptized Jesus "to fulfill all righteousness." Jesus understood the situation fully, and using his dialectical craft, approached his enemies in this manner: "John's baptism – where did it come from? Was it from God or from men?"

The chief priests and elders of the temple, who had been preparing all sorts of questions to trip Jesus, were themselves in a Socratic double bind. If they said that John's ministry was from men, meaning God did not send him, then the common people would get angry, for they looked upon John as a great prophet. If they said his calling was from God, then Jesus would say something like this: "Then why did you not believe him?" In the latter case, to say the baptism of John (his message) was from heaven, would contradict all they had said against Jesus. It would ruin their present nefarious plans. They took the only way out. They said, "We do not know." This was humiliating for those gurus who claimed to know it all. Thus the mighty were brought low, their credibility weakened by a carpenter-preacher's two questions of fourteen words. Jesus was one up on them, which only hastened his premature death. He loved life and celebration, but he loved Truth even more, for that is what he was, **Truth.**

His interrogators had previously asked him to tell them what the source of his authority was. He had countered with his questions as a bargain: "You answer my simple query, and I will answer yours." Since they could not or would not, Jesus had no obligation to answer according to the logic of fair exchange. Such irrefutable eristics only exacerbated their wrath

The Herodians were next. They were political Jews who supported Herod, the puppet king and son of Herod the Great. With great carefulness, they approached Jesus flattering him as a man of integrity who "teaches the way of God in accordance with the truth and is not swayed by men." A wise man is always forewarned not only by the character of those who ask, but by their preambles. Their question was a very clever one, given the Jewish obligation to God religiously, and their servitude to Rome, politically: "Is it right to pay taxes to Caesar or not?"

They hoped to show that Jesus was subversive to the Roman rule, for surely he would place God first. Jesus often used visual aids, and he opted for that method this time. He asked for a coin and then put a question: "Whose portrait is this? And whose inscription?" "Caesar's," they curtly retorted. He then gave them an ironic answer, which was neither answered nor answerable:

> *Then render unto Caesar the things that are*
> *Caesar's, and unto God the things that are God's.*

The narrative records the results quite simply: "And hearing this, they marveled, and leaving him, they went away." Who would blame them?

The Sadducees fared no better. They had a basic religious non-faith, like some modern theologians and religious faculty, rejecting the bodily resurrection and even immortality. They asked Jesus a hypothetical question about human relationships in the afterlife with regard to a woman who had married seven brothers. Upon the death of each one, she would marry the next one. Whether she administered poison or was herself a poison is not mentioned, but the ludicrous case invited a strong rebuke, a straight answer, and a question. Jesus went to their own authority, the Torah, and turned it on them.

First, he told them: "You err, not knowing the scriptures." They did not believe in angels including the divine Angel of the Covenant who appeared throughout the Torah. Jesus gets them incensed by saying that humans will be like the angels in heaven, thus attacking another non-belief. Then he asked, "Did not you read it for yourself where God said, 'I am the God of Abraham, Isaac, and Jacob?' God is not the God of the dead, but of the living." The Sadducees were silenced, and Matthew ended the recounting of the encounter by saying, "When the multitudes heard this, they were astonished at his teaching."

It is impressive that the common folk knew clearly what Jesus believed, and understood what he meant. In reflecting on this, I recall an experience with a modern Jewish man who knew the scriptures in the original Hebrew. He was a twentieth-century Sadducee – agnostic at the least, perhaps atheistic. Erich Fromm admired Jesus, and I must say, I admired Erich Fromm. He loved the Bible and used it throughout his writings, particularly in *The Heart of Man* and in The *Art of Loving*. I once drove Dr. Fromm back to his apartment in New York after his lecture at Upsala College in New Jersey on the profound disease of alienation in the heart of man. This became a book by that title. We discussed ethics, maieutics, community action, and the law of God, which he said a man should keep in the event that there is more than this life. That captivated me. What got his interest was that I had resigned my church and went to the marketplace to cook hamburgers opposite Westside High School in Newark, New Jersey. There was no doubt that the untrained chef idolized kids, for at first I offered up many burnt offerings.

I asked, "Dr. Fromm, you don't really believe there is a possibility of immortality, do you?" He responded that it could well be, and since the laws of God were good in themselves, he sought to observe them in case his ideas were wrong. He assured me that a vast number of Jews found no intimations of immortality in the Torah and the prophets. I asked, "What do you think of the teachings of Jesus?" He said that they were the highest moral truth. Then I asked him if he knew that Jesus believed in immortality and the afterlife. He was rather surprised as I recounted the confrontation of Jesus and the Sadducees, with the Exodus quote recorded by Moses, "I am the God of Abraham, Isaac, and Jacob."

It was my turn to be surprised now, for Dr. Fromm took the statement as the author and speaker first intended it, and as the listeners, pro and con, understood it. The humble Fromm was not quite like the Sadducees. He said that he would look further into the matter. Fromm was astonished at the teaching of the resurrection. Let the reader take note of the manner and effectiveness of Jesus' teaching as viewed by a famous thinker such as Fromm. Except for the last chapter, his *Art of Loving* is good for any reader—it helped my dear wife's marriage because it instructed me on the practice of *agape* love.

On two occasions the Pharisees conspired to ask Jesus a question about the law, specifically regarding the greatest commandment. St. Luke gives a classic example of how Jesus employed the Socratic way in ethical and religious teaching. An expert asks what he must do to inherit eternal life.

Since he is a *nomikos,* a teacher of the law, the question is asked back in the usual Socratic style, "What is written in the law?" The retort is a good one – to love God with all one's heart, mind, soul, and strength, and one's neighbor as oneself. They both fully agreed, and so Jesus spoke directly. "Do this and you shall live." However, this idea of love for the neighbor is purely theoretical in the life of the *expertes intelligentiae,* those who say, "Do as I say and not as I do." The Pharisee felt uneasy in the presence of the one who demonstrated the ethic in his own life. Seeing himself in the mirror of this incarnate goodness, he sought psychological relief through another question:

"And who is my neighbor?"

Then Jesus told the familiar Good Samaritan story in a simple manner. A certain man was traveling from Jerusalem to Jericho – the first city blessed, and the second cursed. The first is "up" and the other is "down." He is robbed and beaten, and left half-dead. Jesus was a careful listener, and therefore an excellent respondent.

The word "to reply" is literally to "seize upon" the words of the other. Jesus did that by simply telling the story and then asking another question. He introduced three characters. The first is the priest (*iereus*), a person set apart for service in the temple. His life was more bound to a place than to persons. He passed on by. Next was a Levite, the priest's helper whose duty it was to keep the temple clean and wash the sacrificial utensils. His was a life of mere things. He passed on by, emulating his religious model.

Jesus next uses satire and paradox. The third person was a Samaritan, the despised, inferior, half-breed Jew – the mulatto of that day, rejected by two worlds and belonging to none. It was he who stopped, risking his life in that treacherous place, and gave time and money in helping the injured traveler. It was as though a Protestant clergyman passed by and, being "socially involved," goes to tell the Mayor's Commission on Crime on the Streets, leaving the poor soul bleeding in the alley. A priest comes along and hurries to say a mass for the man. Then an Eldridge Cleaver type comes along and helps him. "What?" reacts the listener, "Leave the Black Panthers out of this!"

Judgment was left to the lawyer, "Which of the three do you think was a neighbor to the man?" As prejudiced as he was against Samaritans, and as much as he would defend the keepers of places and things, he was forced to yield the inexorable answer, "The one who showed mercy toward him." Exit Carl Rogers and enter William Glasser again, giving a positive and direct communication, "Go and do the same."

Here in combination are many maieutic factors masterfully demonstrated: the question answered with a question; seizing on the observation of character in the other; eliciting another question; the indirect communication through story; the ultimate question and a confession begrudgingly extorted, yet verbalized, thus opening the possibility of self-knowledge. Upon the accession, the teacher gives a mandate to go beyond words – "Take a little love out on your neighbor," as Jackie DeShannon sings in "Put a Little Love in Your Heart. The Westside jukebox received many a quarter to hear the bad and the good – "The Eve of Destruction" by S. D. Sloan *and* Bert Bacharach's "What the World Needs Now Is Love, Sweet Love" (sung by Dionne Warwick). Can you imagine how that jukebox paid for my ministry as I, merely playing Socrates, asked: "How can you put a little love in your heart?" and "Why are we on the Eve of Destruction and what can you kids do about it?" What serious fun!

The teaching of Jesus was effective, for it remains throughout literature and in the vernacular of everyday American life. When I was mugged while on an errand of mercy in a northern city, the headlines said, "Good Samaritan has a fight on his hands." In the New English Dictionary, the Good Samaritan is "one who sacrifices to help another."

Jesus had confused all his conspirators – Herodians, Sadducees and Pharisees. Then, to add insult to injury, this religious Columbo asks them one more little question: "If the Messiah is the descendent of David, how can David call the Messiah his Lord-Jehovah at the same time?" They did not know, thus displaying a humbling ignorance; or they would not venture a possible answer, for in the latter case, it would give Jesus authority beyond his obvious humanity. One must say obvious, for within a few days, he was bleeding and dying on a cross between two thieves. This surely would prove he was not God as he apparently claimed.

As in the case of Socrates, such dialectical success cannot be allowed to live. The question mark looks like a noose but it invites the cup or the cross. The Greek was rewarded with the cup, and died among friends. Jesus was rewarded with a crucifixion, and died among enemies. As in life, so in death, the maieutic person is that Third Fool who not only asks the existential questions, he *is* the question. The apostle Paul confessed to the Corinthians that the whole Jesus affair was a puzzle: "A stumbling block to the Jews; foolishness to the Greeks."

CHAPTER 5

TALE OF TWO CITIES: THE CITY OF GOD AND THE CITY OF MAN

My name is Ozymandias, King of Kings. Look on my works ye mighty,
and despair! Nothing else remains.
Round the decay of that colossal wreck, boundless and bare,
the lone and level sand stretches far away.
Percy Bysshe Shelley

W here may one best learn about the triumph and tragedy of man? Is it not the city? Where does one find art, music, architecture, technology, medicine, religion, law, government, and great educational institutions, all interconnected by intricate systems of economics, transportation, and human interface? In a sense, the city is one vast organism, the Leviathan reflecting man as a physical being, to use the imagery and model of Thomas Hobbes.

Yet again, where may one find heaped into one vast pond of profound despair such a concentration of hurt and hate, destitution and depravity, with ever-deepening discouragement as to the human condition? There should be bright and beautiful hope in the light of man's achievements in the *polis*, yet instead, we find the clearest testimony that man has lost his way, and that the city is full of dead-end streets. What should have become an idyllic Utopia, each time man builds his Babel, somehow becomes a dysfunctional Dystopia – Utopia upside down. The mighty machine of man's making becomes Frankenstein's monster, the creature becoming a mere cog in his creation. The machine masters men, mangling not only their bodies but their very souls.

Augustine in writing of *The City of God* and *The City of Man* was compelled to deal with the problem of flesh and spirit, and of how the Kingdom of God and the kingdom of man, though inextricably intertwined, are at antipodes to one another. His Platonic dualism somewhat puts asunder what God joined together. The flesh as body, the material as physical, God pronounces as good. The perversions of the flesh, i.e., man's self-centered idolatry and materialism with its insatiate demands, are the concourses for flooding The City of Man with moral pollution, drowning the souls of men in spiritual death.

John Bunyan's *Mansoul* illustrates clearly how the city reflects man. As Diabolus seeks to snatch Mansoul from El Shaddai, a battle of Titans ensues and Man is the battlefield. In all respects, the Divine struggle with the Enemy for the soul of a man is the story of the city multiplied ten thousand fold and more. For those seeking God's reign in the city as their supreme purpose, there should be a dynamic "reverse-thrust" that affects the lives of men, women and children with grace and hope. If the spiritual reign is real, then there should be an effect in the world of men. Where is that evidence of the promised Holy Spirit, in the present Kingdom of God or of the reign and rule of Christ in the Church, by His Word and Spirit, through the Gospel? Should not the Church rise and demonstrate the power of the Kingdom in the City of Man?

The more the true church knows its God, living and moving in His Being – infinite, eternal, and unchangeable in wisdom, power, holiness, justice, goodness, and truth – the more it is inevitably impelled into the world. It must be asked in each generation: "Does the Church know God or merely know about him?" In the midst of the mightiest kingdom on earth, Daniel boldly affirmed, "those that *know* their God stand firm, and take action."

In other words, the test of true religion is firmness of character and commitment to truth is to speak as did Luther to the ecclesiastical kingdom of Rome and the Holy Roman Emperor: "Here I stand; I can do no other, God helping me!" The valorous action and gargantuan labors of Luther for the Reformation of the Church have scarcely been equaled. Some regretfully are standing firm, though not for essential truth. And if they do, they seldom back their stand with any real action. We can only pray that God would give us a dozen Luthers for such a time as this. Pious popcorn religion and teleglitz will do little, if not less than little, to make a difference in the city. Luther said it well: "If I profess with the loudest voice and clearest exposition every portion of the Word of God except precisely that little point which the world and the devil are at that moment attacking, I am not confessing Christ, however boldly I may be professing Him. Where the battle rages, there the loyalty of the soldier is proved; and to be steady on the entire battle front besides is mere flight and disgrace if he flinches at that point." Francis Schaeffer from *Luther's Works*, Vol. 3, pp. 81f.

To the scholastics of our age, the philosophers and theologians, this essay is a call to the city. The magnificence of man created and creating, with the drama of his bold rebellion against all that is good, is best described, diagnosed and prescribed in the *megalapolis*. Today, we must move *academia* to the University of the City, to the marketplace of men and ideas. This is where history is born and lives – and dies as well. We must abandon our Ivory Towers of inert ideas and return to the *agora*, letting truth run free. Wisdom must again cry on the street corners, in the modernity of the malls, and into the dead-end alleys of urban life, until the high walls of deep despair come tumbling down. Socrates said that "the unexamined life is not worth living," and this is the bare existential truth. Without real honest-to-goodness living, candid, vulnerable, flexible and teachable, there is no truth walking the streets. And yet as we have said in another place, an equally inescapable truth is that "the unlived life is not worth examining." But pulp magazines and TV keeps us updated on the froth of the ongoing *unreality* show. The safe houses of business and government, church and school, and the linear, lifeless, witless mainframe of mere electronic information, or even one's personal computer – these can only become mausoleums for technocrat corpses or store window manikins, mere life forms, some of them headless.

There is a tragic lack, for modern man, in the exercise of the human soul—that which is separated by a vast abyss from the incomparable person, the *imago dei*, created to reflect Something Greater. The city is the environment which ruthlessly examines life. It is the place where life can be lived in a richness that makes it worthy of that examination. It would be well to comment on the use of the term city here. The Latin word, *polis* (as in North Pole), from which we get politics and police, shows that the city is the center of things. Thomas More could be locked in the Tower of London, cut off from the court and commerce, but the life of London was in him. Therefore from the pitiless prison he spoke with prophetic power to the pathetic King Henry VIII. He was at the center of the moral dimension of the city, for Absolute Truth is the essence of the city. It is a living, moral organism, inescapably accountable to the Living God.

For eleven years that tinker's son, John Bunyan, was imprisoned, but he was full of the city of man, and ably described every snare, slough, fool and sage in the pilgrimage from the City of Destruction to the Celestial City. He was desperately alive in it all, and his book has been the most read in history except for the Bible.

There are people who live in the city, yet whose entire life is lived out somewhere else – a nether world of nothingness, devoid of meaning. However, there are those who live in small towns like Hereford, Texas or Benton, Arkansas, who are fully cosmopolitan, although possessing unique and peculiar smells and accents. Psychologically, one must move from Thoreau's vacuous Walden, a two-year dream child, to the real world. That noble dreamer's only problem was that he had to live with *himself* there.

One must be more fearful of the unlived life than the risks of reality in the city, existing in both triumph and tragedy. The question we ask here should follow that of Francis Schaeffer, "How shall we then live?" The next question is a moral consideration in our spiritually destitute Western Society: "Where do you really live?" If you say New York or Alma, Georgia, it matters not. The question is, "Do you live in the city?" It is not a location; it is an *ethos,* a lifestyle of relevance. Did not Jesus pray that His people should remain in the world, i.e., the City of Man, and not be taken from it? The problem is never the man in the world. The problem is with the world in the man. Perhaps we should agree with Major Ian Thomas that

God's great problem is not getting man out of hell into heaven, but getting himself out of heaven into man and into action in the world.

Any one of our great American cities is greater than Babylon in wealth and weaponry, population and power. Yet each seems to be disintegrating, as did Babylon. The earthquake fault, which brought San Francisco to physical ruin at the turn of the last century, is scarcely comparable to the moral abyss existent now through human fault as we now live in a new millennium.

Look at Mexico City, Rio, Brasilia, or westward to Hong Kong, Peking, Singapore, Tokyo, Delhi, Mumbai, and Kolkata. Tokyo and Mexico City have surpassed 30,000,000 persons. These cities are where mere men pass laws and judgments, yet they are signs that point to the mighty, awful judgment of an infinite and holy God, before whose throne heaven and earth will flee. Was it not Pascal who said, "The city reflects the law of God?" And surely this is so, in ways both negative and positive.

It is a no-brainer. Suppose everyone in the city kept the commandment, "Thou shalt not steal." Consider the millions upon millions of dollars expended on police, jails, hospitals, courts, lawyers, probation and parole programs, private security guards and electronic security systems, not to mention the millions spent in replacing that which is stolen. One can readily see how simply keeping one law would bring unparalleled prosperity and peace. What if "Thou shalt not commit adultery" were honored in loving conjugal fidelity, or even if it were dutifully kept in a less-than-loving relationship? If the people of the *polis* kept this most sacred and difficult contract of marriage with the personal dimension demands it makes of us, would not the city attain the quintessence of moral beauty? Think of the blessing to the nation and its children, and those generations yet to be. The city is obviously the very center of national societies and what the *polis* is, the nation is; what the nation is, the world is.

Utopia: Man's Quest for Eden

Thomas More made a grand pun indeed when he coined the word, "utopia," which means either good place or no place. Although he hoped for the good, perhaps his realism said that there was no such place. Yet he seemed to write with hope against hope that man could somehow measure all things and fill his measure. Let us look at More's ideal society for man's hope as he begins and ends with himself. It is the illumination of such classics that assists our modern phlegmatic minds, far distanced from literature by time, television, or passive education – or perhaps all three. And for post-post moderns, texting, twitter and more.

In Utopia it was recognized that there would be war, but mercenaries were hired to fight. It was much cheaper, and Utopia lost none of its valued citizens. If such aliens were killed, then there would be fewer greedy people in the world. If they won, the mercenaries would merely receive money, which was not a necessity for Utopians. The children were trained in the unique value system (whether primeval or advanced, one does not know) of using golden washbowls and silver urinals. They played marbles with emeralds and diamonds. They could only laugh at foreign ambassadors parading through Utopia with their baubles – "priceless" rings, bracelets, crowns and earrings. What a unique ghetto, unconcerned for the outside world and not affected by it in the least!

There were seven principal cities on the island, about the size and shape of a modern *megapolis* named Long Island. The communities within each city were manageable, with thirty families on each street, fifteen on each side. These groupings had frequent celebrative experiences of eating together, with music and fun, and interesting learning times always including the young. Thomas More pictured the farmers calling on the good city folk to drop everything at harvest-time and go help in the country. Such an optimistic view of human cooperation is surely a no place!

It is heartening to note that the University of the Nations in Hawaii is designed after this pattern, from where it sends its students to the ends of the earth with the Gospel and skill. Something less than Utopia, but it is working because it operates in the real world and is established on the bedrock of Redemption.

My point here is that if man is to have any hope, he must first recognize his hopelessness. *Homo sapiens* are a fallen species, and as such, lack the wisdom potentially derived from a fear of God or from a sense of moral accountability to him. The proper extension of the Reign of God on earth demands something radically redemptive – a new kingdom of the heart. In the long haul, for life as we know it, there are no *Walden*-like escapes – nature walks by the pond are accessible to a chosen few.

Jacques Ellul in his exhaustive and chilling critique, *Technological Society*, gives a formidable argument that man is trapped in the draconian monster of his own making, and there is no escape. He comments that there are three possibilities that are beyond the parameters of mere sociological analysis. The first is some universal cataclysm such as a nuclear holocaust; the second is that man experience a moral change, a renewal within himself; the third possibility is something wholly outside of rational scrutiny, a superior force above and beyond what we know in our closed system – a *noumena* interposing itself or himself in our space and time.

One can readily see that this off-handed statement in Ellul's preface is quite theological, dealing with soteriology and eschatology. John's Gospel and Revelation call for serious study in this regard. It is very sad indeed that man does not look for some answers beyond his closed cultural cocoon. He is locked into "the uniformity of natural causes in a closed system" says Francis Schaeffer in *Escape from Reason*.

Augustine saw that the City of God was a Kingdom ever eternal and present – over, under, and within. It was *now and not yet*. Rome was quite temporary, and would fall of its own weight. She developed from necessity because of the unifying direction of human affairs, because she was located at a juncture of cultures and trade routes, and because there was a demand for goods and the freedom to exchange them. Rome also had popular education and assembly, with just laws of distribution and an elected Senate. There was also a convenient religious scheme of things helpful to the state – a civil religion. Yet its continuance is as ephemeral as the myth of Romulus' birth or Jupiter and Juno founding Rome on its seven hills. That kingdom intersected with the present Kingdom of God (the Church) for over 500 years with world-changing effects. Imagine two circles intersecting, one *the City of God* and the other *the City of Man*. The ellipse is the Church, living in both kingdoms, and that is as it should be. The ellipse, if it grows into God, will grow into the world, thus enlarging the Kingdom or Reign of God on earth.

We see the cosmic Kingdom as eschatological, coming at the end, yet always present in the world through the Church. The Lord's Prayer speaks of the Kingdom coming on earth as in heaven. That is the eternal **now** of the Gospel; and the everlasting tomorrow unveiled with Christ at the summing up of all things in Him, according to the Bible.

The City of Man pragmatically tests the validity of the Law and the Gospel, and is the best recruiting ground for new citizens for the City of God. These will be the innumerable multitudes dwelling in the future heavenly Jerusalem, which will necessarily enter history, perhaps in this century of clashing civilizations. After all, where would we find the people to populate a city 1500 miles long, 1500 miles high, and 1500 miles wide? Only through the Gospel can one live in and beyond the City of Man with the People of God.

Even so, Lord Jesus, come quickly!

CHAPTER 6

ENTROPY: THE CHURCH FROM BIRTH TO DEATH

When Truth Has Fallen in the Street

The writer of this monograph has had a part in developing several churches. Some were ethnic and multi-congregational. Others were developed in such places as the inner city, a university campus, and even on beaches. He has seen some old ones revive and some die. His experience is mostly in the hard places where few dare to go, and he claims all too little "success" and no easy solutions. We see again and again that the local church runs down, which is ultimately reflected in dying denominations. One historic denomination, a leader in the founding of the American Republic, is losing over 40,000 members a year. God looks with apparent indifference on his people when they neglect the first principles of holy obedience and love in the Gospel, while creating their creedal, cultural and comfortable idols.

Entropy is another word that may be used for the *Second Law of Thermodynamics*. In the physical universe it is observed that the cosmos is running down, pointing back to a beginning of great power and purity. Jeremy Rifkin, by no means a friend to Christian ideas until lately, has written a book entitled *Entropy*. He sees the same descending principle in society and no longer hails a humanistic or a heavenly *Utopia*, but calls for a realistic assessment by modern man. He does not call for escape, but for a realistic courage to take action even if doomed to failure. That grand humanist Erick Fromm, in *The Revolution of Hope* said that if there were but one green blade of grass left upon the earth, he would cherish it and guard it with his life. The Church has historically experienced the "Second Law of *Unspiritual* Dynamics." We see repeatedly that the Church (worldwide) and the church (local) also plunge downward. God looks with diffidence on his people when they neglect the first principles of holy obedience to the Gospel and incarnate love. Modern/Postmodern Man creates his own material and cultural idols, and becomes like them. From Joshua to Judges, from Jerusalem to Corinth, from Ephesus to Laodicea, we see the problem, and our hearts are dismayed. Man, as the measure of all things, does "that which is right in his own eyes, and there is no king . . ." The Lord Jesus must surely be weeping over his Church.

It is of little comfort as we bash the homosexuals because it turns out that the sin of Sodom was not sodomy, but the same sin as Laodicea and modern evangelicalism. Hear the weary prophet giving God's Word to his contemporaries:

Now this was the sin of your sister Sodom: She was arrogant, overfed and unconcerned; she did not help the needy; she was haughty and detestable before me. Therefore, I have done away with her!

Ezekiel 16:49, 50

Sounds like John's description of Laodicea, does it not? Revelation 3:17-23. The implication is a "how much more" argument from the lesser to the greater. The more light, the more judgment. Let us look at some historic principles and in that light search our hearts and repent of our sophisticated Christian sins.

A Northern Look: Two Generations Ago

For well over one hundred years, churches in America have been facing the problem of mobility as new waves of different cultures have engulfed their once ethnically, socially and economically *"unicultural"* communities. All too few churches have ever been prepared for the change, and the general pattern is as follows:

- Three or four abortive attempts are made to reach the community, neglecting sound biblical and sociological principles with a combination of cowardice, classism, laziness and the incestuous, ingrown programs.
- This is inevitably followed by a gradual pessimism, producing a bastion, "hold-the-fort" complex.
- Finally, the building is sold to anyone who can pray and pay, no matter what the principles in the dedication of such holy ground had originally been. No one could read the dedication prayers of such church sanctuaries without weeping when the final flight to the safer reaches of suburbia has been consummated, and the church has built bigger and better barns. One church analyst said that the church has these three phases: **Incline,** with focus on *people*; **Recline,** with the focus on *programs* (slowly dying but oblivious to coming oblivion); **Decline,** which is a seemingly incurable financial crisis, usually centered on *property*. This latter is a clumsy juxtaposition of many chiefs and few Indians.

Newark, New Jersey was once one of the great Presbyterian and Dutch Reformed centers in America. Such names as Tennent, Witherspoon, Frelinghuysen and Stuyvesant were common in the church and the body politic. George Whitefield preached in Newark with powerful effect. The Protestants became the strong upper class and controlled the power structure. Then waves of immigrants began to fill the houses left behind as the upward thrust moved the former residents into Morris and Mercer Counties, and to other states as well. Some houses in the Ironbound Ward of Newark first had Dutch and then English inhabitants, then German; next came Italian (the Irish came at the same time to the neighborhoods), then Polish-Jews, and next Puerto Ricans and finally the Portuguese. In the more recent years assorted African Americans, Muslims, Lebanese, Asians (boat peoples included) and Haitians came pouring into the area.

Wilbur Chapman, a Presbyterian minister and associate of D. L. Moody, came to Newark *circa* 1905. He brought a team of eighty ministers and laymen, organizing a united mission to all the churches in the city, preaching in taverns, streets, and burlesque houses, and holding simultaneous meetings in eighty churches. The effect was so great that in Atlantic City the *ministerium* reported in 1905 that there were but five non-professing Christians in the city. The Holy Spirit changes were evident for over twenty-five years in the general culture. But alas Newark became one of the most destitute and desperate cities in America. It led in almost every statistical category: abortion, drugs, alcoholism, violent crime, under-employment, marginal education and substandard housing, not to mention infant and maternal mortality rates, roach and rat infestation, fires, and so on. The first decade of the twenty-first century, however, found a new life and spirit, a dedicated Mayor and the building of a performing arts center and a sports arena second to none.

On Palm Sunday, 1957 a naïve twenty-eight-year-old Southern Presbyterian pastor preached his first sermon in the magnificent First Reformed Church in Newark (seating 1200). He fondly hoped to do a significant work in three years, and go back South where he belonged. The Classis of Newark gave him a thorough examination in theology, and then raised the question: "How will a white Southerner view the *colored* community? Will you not fail to minister to them by neglect or perhaps by a bigoted attitude?" His answer was as simple as his naiveté: "Fathers and brethren, I don't believe in integration and I don't believe in segregation! I believe that a church should simply minister to its own community, and through the power of the Gospel and by the unity of the Spirit reflect the community – whatever is there."

The outcome was that a culturally ignorant Southern boy became the founder of the second Hispanic Reformed congregation in the whole denomination and received the first Afro-American members in the New Jersey Synod. If there was some great principle at work, it was hidden. Now we know that even feeble prayers, when wedded to God's wise Providence, produce his gracious "in spite of" blessings.

Also during this period the sociologically ignorant preacher developed the evangelism methods learned from his father and refined them in the fires of Newark. The old First Reformed Church led the Classis in professions of faith in Christ because it espoused an attitude of "we will come to you" rather than "you come to us." Then while preaching for ten days in a mill village in Scottsdale, Georgia, he planted these principles where they were cultivated by Kennedy Smartt, who, in turn, taught D. James Kennedy, and it was he who had the faith and the gifts to develop *Evangelism Explosion*, which now has an international ministry, far beyond the struggling urban ministry in Newark. As of this writing it is operating in 209 nations, including North Korea. No one was more surprised than the young minister at this, for he only passed on that which he had received, and it certainly fell on fertile soil.

Providence North and South: Nothing Is Done in a Corner

But where did these ideas really begin? Where had they been born and nurtured, before coming to be tested in the northern wilderness? It was in Miami, Florida where an earthy preacher worked with people, identifying with them where they were, asking them those evocative questions that midwifed their thoughts and feelings, and thereby opening the way to presenting a clear Gospel with helpful, simple illustrations. Eight churches and many ecclesiastical grandchildren sprung from those deeply-sown Gospel seeds. One is constrained to cry out, "Lord, do it again!"

There is no doubt that the astute observations of Arnold Toynbee are at work in the Kingdom. The *splinter theory* states that what may grow slowly and incubate in one culture or group may fester and grow exponentially in another with just a "splinter" of an idea entering into that *foreign* body. The Macedonian call to Paul in Asia Minor brought mighty Gospel growth in the Western culture even as the Marxism of Germany found its real home in Eurasia. The Church must realize that what happens in the small towns may affect the city, and what happens in the city may affect the suburbs – that the "twain shall meet" perhaps on the other side of the globe.

Wilbur Chapman's great success in Newark took place before the Protestants said, "We must run, we can do no other." The political system was eventually left to the Irish and Italian Catholics, and the educational system was more parochial than public. It was vast cultural changes bringing alien peoples to the city that disturbed the comfortability of those "at ease in Zion." The new demographics uncovered the true heart of the local church – whether she was committed to be "All things to all men that by all means (she) might save some."

What was I to do, as the church at large had given up on the city? I presented to the Classis the concept of developing a sister church under our session, in the suburbs; the idea being that the collegiate system of mutual support from suburbia, where many of the Reformed folks had moved, would bless the city. The Classis did not support the church plant on financial grounds just as they had decided with the Hispanic ministry proposal. The Consistory of First Reformed Church undertook the Hispanic work anyway, since it did not need much money. They simply used the Gospel, and trained a highly-gifted though undereducated young layman, whom the Classis wisely ordained. Today *La Iglesia Reformada* is still extant after forty years.

In the historic suburb of Springfield, where a core group of fifty dedicated Christians had already gathered and were worshipping together, The Ukrainian Orthodox Church offered the use of their property, but the elders obediently complied with the Classis and this church did not get planted. Later, however, a lease was signed for two acres with a chapel and a residence. Today there stands a fine church building and a congregation of three hundred members. An opportunity had been lost to one group and been taken on by another. Even there entropy has entered, for at one time it had consisted of seven hundred members. Incidentally a young evangelist we recruited and who lived on the property then leads a worldwide movement in open-air evangelism and church planting.

The young minister at First Reformed Church had gotten older and more realistic. He saw that the cultures of the church and the city had little in common, and something had to be done – something that wasn't being done needed to be done to get the job done.

He had gotten the idea (while preparing a sermon titled, "Launch out into the Deep" from Luke 5) of opening a luncheonette by a large urban high school. He drove by the place and large bright letters on the window read, "LUNCHEONETTE FOR SALE." Here was the key to the culture – reaching the people where they were. The pastor resigned from the church, acquired the luncheonette, and became sociologically educated. In 1967 he was at the very heart of the conflict known as the Newark Riots, which were far more economic than racial. Yet, racism created the vast economic divide.

It was an education in war, economic war, where, because of our history and racism, some did not have equal justice or opportunity. The Afro-Americans who had moved out to Montclair did not riot. It was the poor in the city that did. Newark lost 400 churches over the last century. Quite a few new ones started up, mostly storefront churches with no connection to the city – just locations. If it is not too late for Newark, for the Gospel lives, we may yet learn much from past history as you will see later in the chapter.

Perhaps all of that was a testing ground for church re-planting in Miami, Florida in the 1980s. It was then that this writing was first submitted to the sessions of two very special and beloved churches of that city. One church expired; the other closed its doors in the next decade. They were good folks but on the whole, Presbyterians (mainline Anglos) are ill-prepared for the gargantuan cultural changes in our nation. However, instead of fixing blame, let us learn our lesson. NOW!

Understanding Entropy and the City Church

Let us now observe the birth, happy childhood, exuberant adolescence, and grand maturity of the local church. When one sadly asks, "Why did it die?" . . . he is all the more pained to discover that over 50,000 churches in America are listed in the same tragic, ecclesiastical necrology.

The Birth

Most churches at their birth are a homogeneous, one-culture, one-class, one-language group. People tend to build clubs, societies, and churches around their common roots and class. Jesus began mostly with Galileans. Some modern church planting and church growth strategy is unbiblical, slanted toward the upper classes that can:

A. Pay their own way
B. Pay for the "under-class" churches, and feel good

The first is the general practice, and the second rarely happens. Even starting a black upper-class church to minister to the "poor" blacks is doomed to vast failure. Professional black Christians are like white Christians – basically seeking "peace and affluence," as is so aptly described by Francis Schaeffer in *The Church at the End of the Twentieth Century*. Middle and upper-class evangelicals are little different from the Joe Pagans. They are self-interested, self-contained and myopically locked into their one-culture group. Many such churches are very busy and active, and seem to be healthy, but there are very few conversions. A. W. Tozer said that if the Holy Spirit left such churches, they wouldn't know it for two years.

Childhood and Adolescence

The formative stage determines a healthy adolescence. In this period, habits of worship, stewardship, caring, personal disciplines, prayer, and witnessing are developed, together with elders who, modeling after Christ and the pastor, fulfill their vows faithfully. The church grows from infancy to adolescence, breaking the crucial barriers of 100 and 300 members. From that point, there is enough money and means to keep on growing if the community is growing. The Miami churches, Baptist and Presbyterian, grew phenomenally during the depression and after the mega "Twenty-Six Hurricane," Miami lost one-third of its population. The moving of the Spirit consisted of pastoral, house-to-house, church-wide and community-wide evangelism. There was a remarkable unity among the churches, as they found common cause in the Gospel. Jesus prayed that when they were one as he and the Father were one, the world would believe that the Father sent the Son.

Generally, America has one-culture church growth with an upward mobility that soon forgets the "rock from which it was hewn." Already the inexorable principle of **entropy** is at work. The healthy church, however, reaches the people of the same culture and ethnic group, then the class above (where they are going), and the class below (where they had been). The class diversity may open the door to ethnic diversity if the church is loving and obedient to the Great Commission, exhibiting its identity in God. This gracious blessing is a rare phenomenon. One is profoundly stirred and equally envious in reading that shining essay on the real "First Church" in J. B. Phillips' introduction to *The Young Church in Action*.

Maturity

The healthy church generates missions to other groups through giving and sending its own sons and daughters. It is secure enough to deal with the embarrassing social diseases of drugs, alcohol, immorality and other such things across the street or the tracks. Its members help the elderly and the poor. They work in missions and jails, and take time to labor overseas. It is at this point that some of the finest examples of the Spirit's creative work in the Church begin to falter, and eventually fail. Why does the entropic disease affect this healthy specimen with its growing budget? Here are the maxims of Dr. E. I. Rhone.

Maxims of Atrophy and Negative Growth

The American Evangelical Experience

Let us review the *schemata* of Ken Priddy pictured in his revitalization seminars. Think of a trapezoid, with a wide base and a narrower top. Let us revisit this graphic and simple *schemata*. The *incline* on the left of our trapezoid is the growing church whose focus is on **people** – the community. Secondly the top of the trapezoid is the church on *recline*, where the church is turning inward, with the excitement and busyness and joy of **programs** that meet the insatiable tastes of the postmodern consumer church. Without knowing it, they are becoming *entropic* – having forgotten about the "other sheep . . . not of this fold." The entropy is fully evident with the right side of our figure. The church is on the *decline* and the focus in now on **property.** Older folks, energy diminished, seek to survive by clinging to the non-functional structures left them, and having almost more committees than they do people.

- Growth will continue at various rates if the church adapts to and reflects the culture around it, whatever the changes in class or ethnicity, including language.
- Growth will decelerate, stop and become negative as the culture changes when trans-cultural leaders have not been developed by the seminaries and "Barnabas Christians" (the bicultural Hellenists) are not trained in the congregation. The church speaks on this wise: You all are welcome to come and fit into our language,

culture, forms and lifestyles. How distant from the condescension of God "stooping to behold the things of earth," in a manger.

Incarnation is not an option. It is the Risen Lord being himself on earth in terms of his Body, the Church.

What Is the Entropic Process?

The entropy principle states that the usable energy in the universe once expended can never be re-used. Technological society by its mindless environmental stewardship is now exhausting energy exponentially, and the ineluctable result will be a cold, dead earth.

Paul told Timothy to guard the faithful word faithfully committed to him. How was it to be done? It was a stewardship not of using but of giving, "to faithful men who will teach others also." A cold, dead church is the result of poor stewardship of the Gospel in disobedience to Christ's call to preach to all nations (Gr. *ethne*, thus ethnic groups) by the only renewable energy source in the universe – the Spirit of the living God.

The United States is 6% of the world's population, and yet 80% of the world's resources are expended by happy Americans each year. The American church is an outrageous reflection of the same mindset, and the result is as Jesus said: "The love of many shall wax cold . . . then shall the end come."

Let us look at the process and identify our place in the picture of the dying church.

- The members get older and cease to have children (biologic, Dutch evangelism ends). Gospel evangelism to the community has long ago died out. Sometimes neighbors think the church is closed.
- Time, distance, and energy become factors and the actual labor in and for the church diminishes. There are so many elderly and infirm that it is a full-time job caring for these, a privileged responsibility, of course. But this is the time for expanding to the local, changing community. More and more energy is expended in maintaining the building, which is highly valued, often beyond reason and above the eternal souls of men. Quite often, giving increases at home and abroad, creating a false comfort. It becomes

increasingly harder to have covered-dish dinners with a common sharing. Catering is the way most fellowship meals are now enjoyed, which is understandable due to time, two-job families, and distance. Koinonia (fellowship) becomes less intimate, and close bonds are all too rare.

- Geographical and Upward Mobility mean that the young adults, the hope for the future, have moved to other areas, where loyalty is seldom over five miles long. A bright hope in the twenty first century is that there is a renaissance in the center cities.

We have observed entropic churches seemingly turn around by the following means, but more often than not, such growth cannot be sustained:

1. Excellent, attractive programs with the best of Madison Avenue publicity, serving targets such as singles, families, youth, athletes, etc.;
2. A charismatic leader, an entertaining expositor or a great English accent may hold the crowd;
3. The joyous charismatic assembly, untenable for some communions, but dynamic and not to be ignored;
4. The carnival, the miracle, or Christian entertainment atmosphere for curious spectator Christians and the world of the young and old media addicts, mindless and clueless but in need of feelings and spiritual highs.

The one thing that has always worked without fail is a heaven-sent revival with confession of sin, and a renewed obedience to the Lord and the Great Commission. This is the best kept secret of the church.

Why should a Church courageously face the changes culturally and ethnically in the community where God put it; and how would that Church have a breakthrough? There is SOMEONE to obey!

- Obey the Great Commandment, loving God as he is and worshiping him with grateful, obedient hearts. (Deut. 6:3-8, Luke 10:25-42) *This is U-preach.*
- Obey the Great Communion, loving one's neighbor in the Church for the sake of the world. (cf. John 17:21, 23, Gen. 12:3, Rev. 5:10) Note the make-up of the church at its birth in Acts 2:1-13, 46, 47.

It is the love for one another in unity that is the final apologetic, as Francis Schaeffer puts it. The accomplished fact of Ephesians 4:1-5 and model of 1 Thessalonians 1 are urged upon us now. *This is In-reach.*

- Obey the Great Commission, taking the Gospel to every person, in every place, sacred and profane. The secret is in making disciples in order to evangelize. A past Moderator (PCA, 1975) James McIlwain told the General Assembly of the Presbyterian Church in America, "You have jumped over Samaria." (Matt. 28:18-20, Acts 1:8) ***This is Outreach.***

When does the church die and become spiritual dust in the ecclesiastical desert?

- When the church is self-satisfied, self-centered, and too comfortable – approaching a Laodicean lifestyle. Revelation 3:14-22 describes a church disturbingly similar to middle-America evangelicalism, confident of a piece of pie in the sky later.
- When the church is motivated by fear, not love (i.e., losing prestige, power, influence, class standing, and buildings).
- When the church has not produced locally transcultural, bold Christian young people and adults, who will and can relate to its changing community.

The Biblical Model

Acts 1:8 shows the direction from local interests to the ends of the earth. The early church was not all that obedient; as Don Richardson puts it, they were the "reluctant church." It was persecution that forced their hand, and it was the laymen who carried the Gospel, not the apostles. In Acts 11:19-25; it was the Hellenists, the bicultural, bilingual Grecian Jews who created the mission breakthrough. Paradoxically, the church they began in a great international city, Antioch, became the key to missions, rather than Jerusalem where even Jesus labored. Thus the significance of renewing the Church in cities like Los Angeles, Houston, Seattle, Newark, New York, Toronto, and Miami is the possibility of a new breed of "Hellenists" – bilingual aliens, who, through the church, reach out not only to their own but multi-cultures.

We also see the value of short-term missions which radicalize the thinking of the normally comfortable "cocoon evangelicals." The youth are now bringing new spiritual breath to many churches by means of mission trips. Barnabas, a two-culture man, was the best the Jerusalem church could send. He had the wisdom to find one better, a tri-cultural Greek-Roman-Jew, Saul of Tarsus, who affected the known world. Our youth need to be raised multi-culturally in an intentional manner.

There comes a time when a church or ministry should move on, shaking the dust off its sandals and reaching out beyond their community. As they go, they will know. When the following attempts have been exhausted, the church should be set free to discover greener pastures:

1. When the church has faithfully gone to its community, and scrapped the "you come (but we hope not) and fit into us" attitude.

2. When it has preached the Gospel wherever people are, clearly and lovingly, with a cultural and personal respect. Aliens and "outsiders" know the difference between authentic love and phony posturing, and are generally sensitive to God's love.

3. When the alien culture is appreciated by Christians vulnerably seeking to understand it, with some seeking to know the language and all showing mercy.

4. When the church has fully sought to be a wise, winning, winsome servant in the community, including caring for the poor. There has never been revival without this.
    Sometimes the poor do not need the church as much as the church needs the poor – to curb its greed!

5. When the church has sought to minister biblically, governed by God's principles, not prejudiced nor yielding to self-serving compromise.

We might also add that the church may quit the field only after it has sought revival and the fullness of the Holy Spirit in humility and faith, and God has refused to hear (is that possible?); when it has trained and recruited transcultural workers and they fail; when outside help has been asked for and was unavailable; when it has served common human needs and was rejected; and when it ministered publicly and from house to house, and there was a general refusal of the Gospel.

A church must examine itself in the light of these things before fleeing from the scene of its birth, happy childhood and exuberant adolescence, settling for death in the city. It was the lamenting prophet who cried pathetically as he noted that " . . . the elders and priests have given up the ghost in the city as they go about seeking meat to relieve their own souls . . . Is it nothing to you, O you who pass by?" (Lamentations 1)

Proposals for the Transcultural Church Context

How to Structure the Responsive Church

1. Leadership must be shared on all levels, without the surrender of biblical or denominational requirements and distinctions. If the cultural idols don't die, the church will!
2. Christian Education must be a joint project, in the language used by the public schools of the host nation (English in America). Adults need to study the Bible in their own language
3. Youth activities are best developed together—they go to school together as noted.
4. Small group structures are "love's necessity" in the church and homes; playing, ministering, praying and eating together should be cherished and frequent enough times for folks to know one another. Without this, there is all too often a deepening alienation and distrust, which is unchristian, unlovely, and circumventing *the practice of Truth.*
5. All groups may be gathered monthly or quarterly for an appropriate celebration – something for all in music and indigenous foods. Celebration together, including the Lord's Supper, is a mighty force for building unity.
6. Finances should be a joint project. Let "the haves" respectfully, not patronizingly, help "the have not's" through a common treasury. This should be done cheerfully and not begrudgingly (the elder brother attitude). Even under the law, the alien had all the rights and privileges of the covenant. No "taxation without representation."

Note: *Where groups are not at home in the larger body or at the church building, house churches are in order, with the sacraments observed with proper instruction and eldership. The early church did quite well for over 200 years in simple home fellowships without public buildings.*

Above all, the three necessities are prayer, Prayer, and PRAYER. Faithful, regular, repentant prayer together must be offered through the

Holy Spirit, with all the church officers and led by the pastor(s). This is the very life of the church, perhaps the hope of America and the world, and indeed a glory to God. An institution is actually "that which stands in for another" – in this case the church institution represents God. Sometimes the church does not look too much like God. Are the people around us blind, or are we blinded to the God above us?

These frail thoughts are not to be considered the last word, and this writer claims some successes and some failures in seeking to follow these principles. Clearly, they are to be obeyed where biblical, and revised where practical and appropriate. Whenever I see the life of Jesus portrayed in the Gospels, I know I have followed afar off. When we see the early church in its naive adolescence, we have the sinking feeling that we have miserably failed in our generation. We have sinned against the Lord and his gracious calling to live out the Gospel in this challenging world, and have blunted his loving purposes and diminished his glory.

If it depended on you and your church to deliver those bought by the Lamb's blood from their bondage in every kindred, tribe and nation, would he be honored and people be reached? If you or your church ceased to exist today, what difference would it make in your community tomorrow? We may as well sing farewell to our church with a small chorus of nice folks with only southern (or western) accents. The truth is you are responsible. Here is how one person prayed about it:

> *Dear Lord Jesus, I cannot be like God and be responsible for this whole world. But my <u>response</u>-ability is simply <u>avail</u>-ability to you to be who you are in terms of who I am, twenty-four hours a day, one day at a time. Forgive me and my church for sinning in regard to its community and your redeeming love so desperately needed, yet not given. Thank you for what you are going to do, beginning with me, through Jesus Christ, the blessed Head of his Church. Amen.*

CHAPTER 7

TRUTH AND WORLDVIEW

Developing a Reformed Worldview in a Postmodern/ Modern World

*T*he only worldview, which is workable, is that which corresponds to reality. Worldviews are simply the philosophical perspective by which one views all of life. It is determined to be affirmed or disaffirmed by what really is. It is existential, but depends on an absolute source. Francis Schaeffer called it "True truth." Hegel, Heidegger, and Hobbes can create a philosophical world that keeps them happy in their "reality," and they invite us into that world. Could we really live in such illusions? Did the philosophers themselves live in the worlds they created? The Greek word for Truth is also translated reality (i.e., that which cannot be forgotten).

> This oral essay on truth was delivered to a church assembly. It is published with the approval of the Office of the Stated Clerk of Central Carolina Presbytery. The author is solely responsible for its contents.

A worldview is simply the philosophical perspective by which one views all of life. It is determined by what one considers as reality. Francis Schaeffer coined the double word for Truth as "True truth." It is true if it corresponds to reality. It is not the truth if it does not.

It may come down to one thing – TRUTH. A worldview will stand or fall based on its relation to God, the universe, society, and the self. The truest Truth is that which manifests the *excellencies of beauty and goodness*. It is practical for life in a fallen world. *The sovereignty of God* may be the watershed of Calvin's worldview, while *the righteousness of Christ* is the center point for Luther. Wesley would look from the heights of *sanctification*, and Jack Miller through *sonship in the Gospel*. I find that *providence* and *the covenant* are twin pillars in my worldview.

The Hebrew word for truth is used to describe the character of God – *faithfulness* is another translation to show that God is true to His character, His Word, His promise. The Greek *aleitheia* is from the negative *a* privative and the verb *lethein*, lit. "to forget." Actually, truth is that which cannot be forgotten. Truth is there *because God is there*. Thus in Romans 1:18 man under the wrath of God must violently wrestle it down, but the very nature of the truth, even on the "scaffold" as in Lowell's metaphor, makes all such efforts vain. There is no *"Escape from Reason."* R.C. Sproul, Jr. presents this dreamlike reverie where he finds himself in an endless labyrinth, and at the point of despair, he comes to two gates. One is shining and large and upon it is the one word, *CHRIST.* The other door, rather lowly, has *truth* written on the lintel. Which would you chose? R. C. says he chose the lowly looking gate of TRUTH, for as one goes through he or she discovers the whole universe of **TRUTH.** But to choose "Christ" might bring one to his death, for there are many christs and only the TRUTH tells us who He really is – fully God and fully Man, our only Lord and Redeemer.

The word "Christ" has a thousand and one connotations because of the perverse nature of man the idolater. Most sects use that word, as do liberals, modernists, Catholics, mainline denominations and the cults that are multiplying daily. Embrace TRUTH and you will embrace the true Christ, and have it all, for "in Him are hidden all the treasures of wisdom and knowledge." Embrace a false Christ, and one loses his way forever in an eternal labyrinth of darkness. I was at Covenant College in 1971 for the opening salvos of the L'Abri bombardment on modern culture. With great curiosity I brought my sociology students from King College. Schaeffer had already penned the first words in his first book, *The God Who Is There.* It was incontrovertible, and yet so simple. Francis Schaeffer, who perhaps first used the word "postmodern" in 1969, was ahead of his time. This statement is more poignant in the twenty-first century than when first published. Changing words and worlds become a marshland.

The present chasm between the generations has been brought about entirely by a change in the concept of truth . . . The tragedy of our situation is that men and women are being affected by a new way of looking at truth, and yet they have never even analyzed the drift which has taken place. Young people from Christian homes are brought up in the old framework of truth. Then they are subjected to the modern framework. (The God Who Is There, p. 13)

We applaud what Montaigne says about it. "When I see Truth coming, I run to her and surrender my sword on bended knee." Modern man engages the truth in deadly combat, and is lost before he begins. The failure of faulty worldviews not founded on "True truth" is inexorable. So what do we mean by "Modern?" Modern man seeks to confine reality to "the uniformity of natural causes in a closed system," as Schaeffer put it. All *isms* except theism are closed systems. Rational is good – John Calvin and Jonathan Edwards present to us a rational theology. But add the *ism* to rational and you have a world shut up to the limited mind of man, further limited by the physical reality of the "given" of his brain. Obviously, Albert Einstein arrived on planet earth with more to work with than Shirley MacLaine – but we look for both to be rational and consistent with their worldview.

Cohabiting cousins Empiricism, humanism, pragmatism, and scientism are honored citizens of this technological age. All postmoderns would cease to exist without the contributions of these as fields of true endeavor and accomplishment. Harry Blamires in one of John Stott's "top five" books, *The Christian Mind,* counts it as a disgrace indeed that we blindly embrace this modern mind by saying, "But science says this or science says that." We Christians have retreated and forsaken the field. It should be that one says, "But the *Christian Mind* says this."

I was a fool about Postmodernism as perhaps some of you were. So impressed by these mindless Sophists and their writings, I felt intimidated. I finally opened the door and looked in. I found there was no one there. Is it really odd that Ronald Nash came to the conclusion that Post-modernism does not exist? How can we be intimidated by this tempest in the teapot, a fad that soon will disappear? We have, unfortunately, authors who are fattening their pocketbooks with modern spoof writing in an objective universe. **The truth will stand.**

The cycle is like this. In three generations of mentors and mentees, Socrates asked the questions, Plato answered them, and Aristotle perfected the knowledge and gave us the definitions. Then Philip of Macedonia asked Aristotle to be the tutor for his son, Alexander. He conquered the world and put a library in every city named after him from Egypt to India. But this knowledge was insufficient for a world of Gnostics and mystery religions – the outcome of the Aristotelian technocrats and other such factors. It would take the objective Truth of the Hebrews and Christians to conquer the Greeks and the Romans.

A peculiar little man who was a seed picker in the opinion of the Greek philosophers was dragged up to the *Areopagus* to give his philosophy. At least they asked, which hardly happens in our modern universities! After a very sage presentation with allusions and quotes from the poets and his own astute observations, he said something that would seem to be off the wall – perhaps even *pre-suppositional.* He said the Athenians were going to be judged by a Man that came out of a grave in a far-off country which they knew little or nothing about. There would be a judgment and the Resurrection Man would preside as Judge. He also blatantly challenged them to repent in the here and now because of this reality. He did not beg. It was God speaking in the imperative.

My question is, "How could a learned man like Paul tell the sophisticated Stoics, Cynics, and Epicureans on Mars Hill that a man was resurrected in Jerusalem, and expect one shred of respect?" It is a very simple answer. **Because it was true!** It was "True truth." It was verifiable in an objective universe, although these particular persons were not in the position to do so, being 1,250 *km* from the *place of the skull.* But Truth has its own inherent persuasiveness, and can be told to anyone, anywhere, and at any time – and hopefully with the wise rhetoric of a Paul. But however clumsy we may be, still better said than not. Actually, it was quite successful if one would consider that it was something like the Cambridge City Council being also the tenured Harvard faculty. Dionysius and others did believe and become disciples.

I was discussing this paper with my colleague Pedro Govantes, Executive Director of the Jonathan Edwards Institute, and asked him his definition of postmodernism. He pictured it to be "thought collapsing into itself"— – a veritable implosion, like a building being demolished. It looks perfectly fine until the dynamite plunger is pushed, and the walls collapse inward in one vast demolition. For postmodernists, there is no more history, no more language, no more literature, and no more philosophy and "truth is lying in the streets." With antithesis destroyed, there is no more thought. It is like leaning on a moving wall that is not there or taking a step in the dark when there is no step. It is nothingness. Why then would we fight that which is not? We have the Truth, we should use it. In short, metaphysically, the postmodern phenomenon is nothing new – it is old world Gnosticism dressed up in twenty-first century clothes. Theologically it is pantheism, philosophically it is monism, existentially it is despair, and intellectually it is irrationalism. The rationalism of Voltaire is followed by the mindless romanticism of Rousseau – one who wrote of the education of children but cared not for his own unwanted son, placing him in a foundling home.

Marcuse in his *One-Dimensional Man* (1954) saw clearly that technological man would be dispirited. It is this vast void that welcomes the New Age with an open and empty heart. Man with his *imago dei* has a God-shaped vacuum (Pascal). Only God can satisfy the heart of man. We are made for Him, and Augustine speaks for the race of men when he says "our hearts are restless until they find their rest in Thee." (*Confessions,* p.1)

If the Church is not there with the Gospel, others will fill their hearts and minds with a hundred damning untruths. Kierkegaard pointed out that the self-centered Danish church would move the society from monarchy to democracy and then sensate materialism, a new god with the same liturgy. He said that the emptiness of the church he loved would someday be filled with a thousand false gods. The scorpions in Revelation, like little dragons, are out of the Pit. When I attended Columbia Theological Seminary (1951), we studied the cults – five or six of them. Now the computers cannot track them as they multiply daily. And how is a worldview tested to ascertain if it is corresponding to reality? Lifestyle is living out one's philosophy – it is worldview with skin on. It usually is sooner than later that the objective universe demands that life and reality correspond, and a tragic toll is ultimately extracted. It is a moral universe, and there are consequences. Say the Lord's Prayer and jump off the Empire State Building. God will look with apparent indifference on such stupidity. Although one thinks he is doing quite well for 110 stories, that last one is quite a jolt! The realm of the mind and spirit in a moral universe is more profoundly serious. A rabid objective atheist who will not jump will fare better. This is not the dour Dane's *leap of faith* but more like Icarus in the flight of a fool in the warm sunlight.

Paul and Paracelsus agree. The greatest reality is love. Wherever we find hope and faith, we will find love (truth) living there. Paracelsus says that *he who knows nothing loves nothing . . . He who understands nothing is worthless, ergo:* If postmodernism, monism and Eastern Mysticism are the *nirvana of nothingness*, then the indispensable necessity of love for a sane society (Erich Fromm) is impossible. Nothing cannot produce something – especially *love*. If love does not exist, neither does God. Oprah's new rage for the New Age is Eckhart Tolle and his New Earth. Here he offers us the privilege of believing in his non-belief that we are becoming one cosmic nothing. There is a value however, and that is $24.95 at Barnes and Noble. He got a name that gives us Meister Eckhart, the mystic and Tolle, strong objective truth.

Note: St **Augustine** (354-430), Bishop of Hippo in North Africa, heard a child's voice say: *Tolle, lege'* (**Take, read**). He walked over to the monastery Bible chained to a wall. It was open to Romans, the first dogmatic theology book. We test both Eckhart and Luther also by the Book.

Dr. Steve Clinton of the International School of Theology spoke of the framework necessary for developing a Biblical worldview. Of his various citations, he prefers the definition of James Sire, editor of many Francis Schaeffer books, in his own worldview offering, *The Universe Next Door*:

> *"A worldview is a set of presuppositions or assumptions which we hold consciously or subconsciously about the basic make-up of our world." (Sire, 1976, p. 17).*

Clinton writes, "Developing a biblical world view is a risky business! If you understand a biblical perspective on issues in life, are committed to God and to His service, and are equipped to serve, He may choose to use you to reach the world. You could become a revolutionary! Let it be, that you may boldly take your stand and do exploits . . . Many of us are committed to God and to His service and are equipped to serve, but must incorporate another element in becoming a revolutionary for God, and that is having a biblical worldview, *i.e.,* a biblical perspective on issues in life." (Unpublished papers, Institute of Christian Studies International, ICSI)

We will italicize a recasting of point 2 with the Reformed distinctive rather than a general statement which references *evangelical* theology. These are the essential elements for a biblical worldview:

1. Knowledge of Bible content;
2. Knowledge of historical theology and Reformed doctrine;
3. Biblical practices integrated into one's life;
4. Knowledge of contemporary cultural issues;
5. The proper biblical response to these issues.

Knowledge of Bible Content

Calvin E. Stowe (husband of Harriet Beecher) introduced John Gillies' biography of George Whitefield to America in 1853 with a stunning essay on the character and lifestyle of the men God wonderfully used in that era of powerful spiritual impulse. Feel the irony as you read, "Although God can do without our intelligence, he can do less with our ignorance."

Schaeffer speaks of the "Reformation memory" disappearing in the twentieth century. Many, many seminary graduates, as you discover in Presbytery examinations, have an abysmal knowledge of the English Bible.

If this is so; what of the people in the pew? In a genial dinnertime with the President and faculty of a blue-blood evangelical seminary, it fell upon me as Dean to lead a Bible game. It did not turn out so well. I asked, "Let us start with Ten Commandments and recite them around the circle."

We could not get a full quote on the second and fourth commandments, nor could they get them in order, and one or two were omitted. I understand that many theological professors, like their secular peers, teach within their narrow spheres, and forget many, many essentials. One of the "Big Twenty" churches of the Presbyterian Church in America sent some elders with this writer to the Cayman Islands to teach Evangelism Explosion and Lifestyle Evangelism. In a casual time before going snorkeling, I thought I would do the pernicious and impertinent "Ten Commandments Game." They scored a five on a 1-10 scale. I would let them neither snorkel nor evangelize until they had memorized the Ten Commandments. **They did, and to this day they thank me for it**!

Let us look at Hosea 4:6-9 to see that there is nothing new and where we are in modern-postmodern times. The prophet says that ignorance destroys God's people and it corresponds with Psalm 11:3 which says, "If the foundations are destroyed, what can the righteous do?" This ignorance is a choice, and therefore God not only takes away the covenant headship of the priest, but God will forget the children of those who forget the knowledge of God. "Like people, like priest" is the result.

I grew up in perhaps the best educated church of the old Southern Presbyterian Communion – a Sunday School of 1200 "scholars" where quarterly exams were given and report cards were sent home – thus 150 biblically astute evangelists went into the ministry in a mere 24 years. The sober truth is incontrovertible. Knowledge in obedient hearts does not blunt evangelism, for in twenty-four years there were 4000 persons who joined Shenandoah Presbyterian Church by profession of faith – just 1000 less than joined the 1200 or more churches of the denomination at the time of this essay being presented!

God's people need to know the truth about themselves, sin, God and redemption, the Christian life and practical religion. The Bible tells about that and more – and with it comes the life-giving Spirit.

Knowledge of Historical Theology and Reformed Doctrine

Calvin informs us in his dedication to the inquisitor, King Francis I, of his reason for writing the *Institutes of the Christian Religion*. It was in order that young students of the Bible would not get lost in Scripture. We might say also that to find "true truth" in the Word one must follow this rule of the Reformer: "To divest myself of all ground of glorying, that He might be eminently glorious." And it was in the historical context of battling for the truth that he and Luther, like Augustine and Athanasius before them, hammered out doctrines to live by through the antithesis of Arians, Pelagians, Arminians and Libertines.

All truth is something to live by and if theology is not practical, it cannot be existentially incarnate and walk out into the marketplace. If "truth claims" cannot be practiced, then they must be deleted with one click unless it is useful to teach truth by antithesis. My question to my brothers and sisters on this fine day would be the same as yesterday or tomorrow. What does Providence have to do with your approach to evangelism or pastoral care? How does the *fall of man* help you understand the tragedy of the world and face reality, especially when implacable evil is found even in the church? How do *evil* and the *sovereignty of God* conspire to spiritually inform the scene of a teen tragedy in an accident or the funeral of a three-week-old baby? How would you handle the thousand and one inequities in the world and those against you if you did not believe in the *Judgment* of God, immanent and transcendent, timely and for eternity? If we truly embraced biblical eschatology, would we not live in the light of *heaven* and *hell* and *the judgment*? Perhaps we are passionless Gospel do-gooders because we do not believe in these eternal verities. George Whitfield said that he lived each day on the edge of eternity, and young Jonathan Edwards put that at the heart of his *Resolutions*.

In other words, how does the Reformed faith shape your worldview and effect the answer to "How shall we then live?" And what of the doctrine of *creation*? Do you take the cultural mandate seriously exulting in the magnificent universe created *ex nihilo* for us to explore or the magnificent world of men and cultures to know? There are classic books to read and the arts to make our minds soar heavenward? The Psalms give us a *world and life view* of worship in beholding *creation* as well as *redemption*.

Give yourself this exercise after you read this essay. List the central Reformation doctrines quickly, and then pick the two or three that govern your *world and life view*. What is missing in your truth framework? Do you have a lifestyle that matches what you profess? What are you going to do about it NOW? By the grace of the Holy Spirit, and the shared life with a spouse and colleagues who love you enough to hold you to account.

Tom Skinner used to explain with tongue in cheek that the reason the "brothers" on the streets of Harlem greet you with "What's happening?" is that they do not know what's happening. Skinner added a positive – they had real questions and many would begin to search theologically for the answers. Does Peter Singer, the ethicist at Princeton, really know what is happening, even to himself? What would he believe about euthanasia when his mother gets Alzheimer disease?

What are the big questions facing postmodern/modern man? What are the worldviews that are out there confronting us? Do we know and understand the people who embrace these worldviews? Are we listening to them empathetically and honestly where they are?

There are some biblical models of men who shaped destiny and what they embraced as the Truth shaped their world and life view, and often cost them their lives.

Abraham, Joseph, Moses, Daniel, Nehemiah, Mordecai, Barnabas, Luke and Paul. And what does church history teach us of Athanasius, Augustine, Patrick, Alcuin (with Charlemagne), Luther, Calvin, John Milton, Whitefield and Wesley? What more can we say of William Tennent and sons, August Francke, William Wilberforce, Jonathan Edwards, David Brainerd, William Carey, Robert Murray McCheyne, Abraham Kuyper, C. S. Lewis, and Francis Schaeffer?

Joseph, without the knowledge of the Holy Spirit as we have experienced Him, knew the presence of God, and therefore could not betray his purity in keeping the as-yet-unwritten Seventh Commandment. He knew the providence of God, and it gave him a pardoning, trusting heart as well as a pure and tried one. Moses was transformed by the calling of the *"God who is there* – the I AM." Psalm 90 shows how the Eternal taught him about time. And Daniel . . . such clarity and wisdom was given him because of his one focus: the worship of God and God alone. The first commandment embraced all holiness and made him holy. He was the Prime Minister of two world empires, and the prophet for the coming Kingdom and the reign of Messiah.

John Piper would suggest to find a biblical and historical model for your life and learn and practice all you can within the limits of God's economy. Should not someone want to follow you as you follow Christ? Who of us would want to be emulated and say with Paul, "Whatever you received and learned and seen and heard from me, do it, and your God will really bless you"? Many of us dare not disciple or be discipled because it will demand a realignment of the great tectonic plates of our inner lives, impacting one another and creating vast, visible character chasms. Our doctrine must conform to reality.

In our masculine setting, we do too easily forget about Deborah, Ruth, Hannah, Esther, Mary, and that remarkable tri-cultural Priscilla? We are Calvinists and some translate it chauvinists. How may one forget Susannah Wesley and Sarah Pierpont Edwards, Edith Schaeffer, or a mother like the one to whom I dedicated this book.

History turns on the character of a Nero or Paul, Churchill or Hitler. Indeed, it was the character of Jesus that qualified Him to redeem us: "*He lived the life that He lived, perfect, that He might die the death He died, to redeem; He died the death He died to redeem, that we might live the life that He lived, by the grace of His risen indwelling life.*" (Ian Thomas, *The Saving Life of Christ*)

Aristotle gave us a model for true communication and if we are to speak to the twenty-first century, we must meet the criteria.

> *Ethos* – The character we bring to our communication – this is the Christian life lived;
>
> *Pathos* – The passion of heart, even to the death! This constrains living it out in the world of men and Ideas;
>
> *Logos* – Knowledge upon knowledge, available for application in the real world. We take the Biblical and Reformed Truth into a world we are learning to know and love with compassion. Then we skillfully confront and pull down the strongholds and build something better: the Church of the Living God.

The Lord said through Ezekiel that the prophets, priests, princes and people were all corrupted and under judgment. God "looked for a man among them to make up the hedge, to stand in the gap . . . and He found none." God is looking for men and women with these three qualifying attributes to speak to this generation. Like Elisha, who never took no for an answer, we must go for it with all we've got. D. L. Moody overheard some venerable old gentleman speak as he was shrouded by a hedge in a garden. One of them said, "The world has yet to see what God can do with a fully consecrated man." Young Moody thought, "I want to be that man!" The rest is history as millions heard the Gospel and multitudes entered into the Kingdom through his simple biblical preaching. His life touched my life indirectly, one hundred fifty years later.

In 1895 Dwight L. Moody came to Savannah, Georgia and with his 300-pound frame of boundless energy, he preached everywhere, sacred and profane, including my grandfather's Seamen's Bethel. Then at the great Independent Presbyterian Church he stepped into the John Knox pulpit, sixteen feet above all contradiction, to preach. With his massive head and beard he perhaps looked like a mighty lion to the son of Halvor Iverson: "Tonight I am speaking about a man in the Bible named Daniel. There is a little boy here with that name," and looking fully in the face of seven-year,old Daniel Iverson he exhorted, "And young man, I want you to be a Daniel just like the one in the Bible." (Ref. to W.T. Iverson, Jr., on the *Memoirs of Daniel Iverson* and the Georgia Historical Society, *circa* 1895.)

My father says that it was then that he was called into the Gospel ministry, as best he can recollect. My call to the ministry simply came as I observed the man in his ministry. He never sought to influence me by word. It was by demonstration that I received the clear call. We tend to reflect the lifestyle and passions of those through whom we are converted, which thus explains evangelistic passion in my father and Billy Graham. That same passion, minus some of the wisdom and gifts those two possessed, burns in my soul, yet I am not consumed.

Finally, let me share with you my critique, simply observed, of those qualities already cited that must be found in the church leadership in this new millennium. Not all will be resident in any one of us fully, but together in the Body of Christ, we can present what we are and have, letting the Spirit of the Living God break and melt, mold and fill as He wills. Aristotle's three attributes for the effective communicator holds true for any generation. With a *Christian worldview framework*, we must undertake the requisite qualities and qualifications.

Ethos: The Character We Bring to Our Communication

Being is before *doing. God who created the universe was simply the Essence, the being, Jehovah.* He had to exist before He created. Jesus spent thirty years simply *being* before He began His brief three-year ministry. But if the axe is blunt, it takes more strength. The holy Son of Man pierced the darkness and was a dividing sword – each word and deed had eternity in it, even washing feet.

It was said of Lyman Beecher's congregation that they "preached" the sermon all week in their lives. Of Robert Murray McCheyne it was said that his "weekdays were the sequel to his Sabbaths" and that "his life was the best exposition of the text." The character of Jonathan Edwards was the foundation for the mighty intellect and the Spirit-given preaching and writing. McCheyne often quoted Chalmers' classic statement that **"A holy man is an awful instrument in the hand of God."**

Luke makes an astute observation when he writes that Barnabas was "a good man, full of the Holy Spirit and faith; and *many* people were added to the Lord" (Acts 11:24). I have shared the way of the Gospel as I learned from my father. In 1969 I received an encouraging note from D. James Kennedy thanking me for being "the grandfather" of his Evangelism Explosion. But something was lacking in my *schemata*. Lately, before beginning these helpful principles in evangelism training, I deal with character (including my own, again and again). He and I agreed that character is the prerequisite. I go to the Sermon on the Mount and we study the "Be-Attitudes" and also find great help in the *twelve signs* of a true Christian as found in Jonathan Edwards' *Religious Affections*. Judgment must begin at the house of God. A witness is a two-edged sword of truth and love.

The Holy Spirit was sent to convict of sin, righteousness and judgment. Without the broken heart over sin, there is no conversion. He convicts of righteousness because Christ has gone to the Father and sent the Holy Spirit (and He is just that!). He creates a holy church practicing the truth and living sacrificially in a broken world. It is now that the church can reveal righteousness to men through both life and the Gospel message. And yet we live as if there is no judgment. Paul declared we must all appear to give account before he spoke of the constraining love of Jesus. His argument from the lesser to the greater was that "Therefore, knowing the terror of the Lord, we persuade men!" (2 Cor. 5:10-21)

What is the character you bring to your wife and children, your church, your community and the marketplace? *We must begin by preaching the Gospel of Law and Grace to ourselves,* by repenting, by heart cleansing, and embracing a perfect alien righteousness, i.e., that of Christ alone, before the Father for us, and then by the Holy Spirit in us as adopted sons. Hallelujah!

Pathos: The Passion of Heart, Even to the Death!

REMEMBER: BEING BEFORE DOING!

Oswald Chambers speaks of how Paul was held as in a vice by love of the Lord Jesus. It was inescapable to be gripped like that. To live in the light of the Cross of the one who loved me and gave Himself for me." He had one holy passion: "The Cross is the center of Time and Eternity, the answer to the enigmas of both. It is there that a holy God and sinful man meet with a crash, and the way to life is opened – but the crash is on the heart of God." (*My Utmost for His Highest*, April 6). If the greatest commandment is broken, yea, even profaned by our narrow doctrinal fetishes and cultural Christianity, it is like binding a risen Lazarus with more grave clothes. Our cultural sin and idolatry bind up new Christians and they become as moribund as we are in our dying institutions. If you are passionless, before you leave your house, don't kiss your wife goodbye. Thus you will kiss your marriage goodbye.

A passionless minister will kiss his ministry goodbye, for he is called to diligently teach the love of God through the law and Gospel, setting life and death before his people and their children in the context of grace. Sadly, when I preach on the covenant and ask for those who have regular family worship to rise – it is a pitiful handful, including elders and pastors, who have double vows doubly broken. If we love not our families enough to faithfully seek their spiritual wellbeing, we will not seek that of our neighbor. We may pull off a well-executed program but without the Spirit's unction it will be devoid of the love of God, and the passion for Christ and His glory, in the lives of men and women and children.

If a liar comes into this room and cries, "Fire, fire," you will not believe him because of his character, and you will continue on as is. But if a man of excellent character strolls in and with a soft library voice says, "The building is on fire," neither will we believe him. And if we do not, we will surely perish in the fire *because he had no fire.*

In a world lost from love, alienated and hurting, modern and technological, postmodern and irrational, we cannot speak a saving word without holy, bold, persevering character. It must be a costly servant love that is evident to all, winsomely calling God's own out of the world and into the strong, loving embrace of Jesus. It must start at home where it is tested with the reality of loving and honest relationships, undergirded by the covenant of grace.

Bettelheim was right in his book on the fragmented and wounded of the world – *love is not enough.* He was right. *It takes knowledge and skill.* This is the content of Greek rhetoric, for "love must speak with wisdom and knowledge" – and that is how truth is spoken.

LOGOS: Knowledge upon Knowledge – Truth for the Real World

We cannot look at the foolishness of man without agreeing with Calvin Stowe, that "although God can do without our intelligence, he can do less with our ignorance." Recently I spoke with a church planter who knew nothing of philosophy and I have known more than one theology student who never had read one book through. Whatever became of *Logos?* Gillies said that the men God used, Methodist Oxfordians such as Wesley Hall, the Wesleys, and Whitefield, were men whose humanist and religious educations were in the service of the Gospel – not sophists, but holy and sharp instruments in the hand of God.

We need to know the "recondite arts" as Calvin said in his observations of creation in his Genesis commentary. Hodge was a modern man who matched the wits of the secular and scientific world of his day. The world has benefited because C.S. Lewis could think, and had a wealth of knowledge in literature, as did Schaeffer in the arts and philosophy, and R. C. Sproul in language, philosophy, theology, logic and rhetoric. Few ever put their minds at the service of God as Jonathan Edwards did, and the labor of it all is beyond comprehension. Although few of us can match such men, we need to have a rational theology on fire. If these men with brains labored so diligently, so must we. Dr. William Childs Robinson said that Calvin did the work of twenty-one eminent professors with a headache for twenty years and disease from head to toe. He gave me a few headaches of my own, but I am eternally grateful that I outlined the *Institutes* twice. Once from compunction, and once for sheer joy – after seminary, of course.

"Dr. Robbie" also exhorted his class, "Men, do not dare to go to a big church as an assistant pastor and certainly not as senior pastor. Take a little church in Mississippi and follow my **5-5-5 Plan**. Study five hours a day, five days a week, the first five years of the ministry, and you will never, never be an empty well to a thirsty people." Hosea writes, "My people are destroyed for lack of knowledge." It lies with the priests and prophets of the church, to give food and drink to the famished souls of postmodern/modern man. I did Dr. Robbie's five-year plan, and never have regretted it. I regret that I did not read more history, science, and contemporary writings and, if only for pure joy, worthwhile novels.

But Newark brought other realities, and I tardily gained a Ph.D. in a great secular university. This gave me a needed discipline and enlarged my borders, even without the help of the prayer of Jabez. I know as never before, thanks to study in a secular university, how very little I do know.

Mercy is what I need, and hard work – "beaten oil for the sanctuary" as McCheyne would say . . .beaten oil burns the brightest and the longest.

Enough of all of this. Let me summarize simply in John 1:14. Our Lord Jesus was God incarnate, full of grace and truth, and so revealed the Father. We have the best plan – *incarnate*! Be there! Show up on Monday. Enjoy living in God's world because He made it and put you there. Jesus did, and they thought He was having too much fun. Such joy was serious to the death, but until then, His life was all grace and all truth. No one will fail in their calling to this postmodern/modern world if mercy and truth meet together in his or her daily life. Surely then shall we see the Kingdom on earth with righteousness and peace kissing each other. Where there is no mercy and truth, there is no goodness and beauty!

A *DENOUEMENT* AND A PRAYER

Let us not forget the words of Anthony to Cassius at the plains of Philippi:

> *We are diminished, and the enemy increaseth every day . . .*
> *There is a tide in the affairs of men, which taken at the flood,*
> *Leads on to fortune;*
> *Omitted, all the voyage of their journey is bounded*
> *by shallows and miseries.*
> *We are now on such a sea afloat, and we must take the current*
> *while it serves, or **lose our fortunes.***
>
> Shakespeare, *Julius Caesar*

Father, Creator of heaven and earth, and Lord Christ, our Savior, let our satisfaction be in You, in Your character and beauty as the infinite and holy God; You did stoop down to behold the things of earth in Your Incarnation; You redeemed us, and poured out Your treasures into our hearts by the Holy Spirit. We know You will be most glorified as we find our chief delight in You alone. Let us daily delight in being available to You, Lord Jesus, to be who You are, Risen Lord, perfectly adequate in terms of who we are, twenty-four hours a day, one day at a time, even to the death or unto Your glorious coming. We thank You ahead of time for the glorious day when all the Redeemed stand together, holy and hilarious, because of Him who procured us that place in His Kingdom in His own blood. Amen.

CHAPTER 8

BIBLICAL ANTHROPOLOGY AND HUMAN-SHAPED EDUCATION: THE INTELLECT AND THE LECTURE

One of the tragedies of modern education is that it views the student as a receptacle to be filled to capacity, followed by an inglorious dumping in some inappropriate manner, such as a short-term memory exam (objective testing). In the vertical transmission mode (piping it down), usually only the brain is involved. Strictly speaking, intelligence is much more than mere rote memorization. It means to "pick and choose between" (derived from *inter* and *legere*). Can one really develop critical thinking without other elements of education? For instance, being "human-shaped" and having social interest in education and the Law of Contradiction is the basis of discretionary dialogue. It involves the term coined by Margaret Mead as *lateral transmission* in contradistinction from one-dimensional *vertical transmission.*

In terms of technology, the sociological prophecy of Jacques Ellul (*The Technological Society*) has come to pass. Students are to become masters of technique, a chip in the computer, a Google slave replacing the galley slave. It is here that a mere mouse discovers a cursory thought of image and word replacing critical thought. Neil Postman in *Amusing Ourselves to Death* gives a devastating literary critique of the same problem—the loss of the text and critical reading. Ellul and Postman though an ocean apart were on the *same page circa* 1964, a turning point decade in Western Civilization.

A decade earlier, Marcuse shows that man in the machine or computer leads to a vacuum in man, humanity de-spirited. A century earlier Marcuse's mentor Kierkegaard predicted the hollow men poetically described by T.S. Elliott a half century later. Can we possibly address the *wasteland landscapes* with "heads of straw"? Modern/postmodern man will embrace a thousand antithetical truths with his vacuous mind and welcomes legions of strange demons that have fragmented whole cultures and nations.

Woodrow Wilson said in his Farewell Address as President of Princeton University that "stuffing the prolix gut" only to "regurgitate the matter" is not education. The sign that true education (remember-L. *exducere*, literally "leading out of") is transpiring is that students talk about things out of class – in the pubs, in the eating clubs, on the green, and in the halls. The lecture is the principal method of the "head stuffing" approach, which leaves us as mere computers, programmed indeed, but with no wild card chips.

It must be remembered, however, that although there are few great lecturers, vertical transmission is indispensable to the academic process, and all teachers should acquit themselves with excellence in presenting material in the monological method, yet with a maieutic (midwifery) cunning that raises questions. Where there are no questions, there are no answers.

The Emotional and the Volitional

Although each aspect of human nature and its educational corollary may be seen uniquely, it is recognized that all of them interrelate in holistic education. We elect here to take various aspects of "man as he is" in tandem, in order to think synoptically of our educational philosophy.

Teaching in a sterile environment safe from the world and its critical issues denies access to the emotions and the will. William James, in *The Will to Believe*, speaks of live and dead options. If there is no real choice presented to the person, the will is left untouched, and there is neither a spiritual nor a moral believing. With keen psychological insight, he shows that the mind (intellect) must fasten itself on an object, for both the emotions and the will are indirectly rather than directly affected.

For example, in the life of Jesus of Nazareth, He went about all the cities and villages teaching, preaching and healing. "And when He beheld the multitudes, He was moved with compassion for them." The Greek word for "compassion" denotes a powerful; gut feeling that moves the person. As He taught people where they were, His will and heart united to call His pupils to action. It was from this point that the mission of the church was implemented as the Lord of the Harvest thrust forth (*ek-ballo*, hurling out as a ball) His followers.

The true educator brings out the love in the hearts of men, models it, and calls them to action. He will courageously present the issues and create the environments for compassion and obedience. The education is for mankind's good by developing better people. Not to do so is to produce mere cogs in the technocratic machine. Technique ("doing it right"), as Jacque Ellul critiques for hundreds of pages in *Technological Society*, can never produce those men and women who live humanely in the world. Adolph Eichmann could certainly "do it right" and in the end did much wrong.

The Physical and the Social

Perhaps I will need forgiveness for this true story, but it is worth the risk. I was teaching sixth graders the Gospel of Luke in preparation for confirmation at Queen of Angels School in the inner-city of Newark. One bright girl, scarcely as large as a first-grader, waved her hand promisingly as I asked, "What are you thankful for today?"

"I'm thankful for my buns!" Monica shouted with knowing conviction. "Your buns?" I shot back incredulously, wondering what sad home environment had warped her little mind. "What in the world do you mean?" "Well, if I didn't have buns, I couldn't sit here in class . . . and if I wasn't in class, I wouldn't be able to learn about God and be confirmed. So there."

Monica had me, and my growing respect for the so-called deprived kids "in the ghetto," as Elvis Pressley attempted to depict, was all the more enlightened. Little did he know. The point is, we are physical beings, and our education needs to take into account that simple reality. In group dynamics we see that group geography, *i.e.*, how we are placed in relation to one another, may allow or hinder intimacy and eye-contact so crucial for the process. Social interest (Adler) is not cherished by straight rows of linear, one-dimension learners. Listening, conversation, empathy and thinking are assisted by conforming the content and purpose of a particular class to the physical and social make-up of man. It is self-evident . . . we don't have eyes in the backs of our heads, do we? It turns out that stomachs and mouths are a major part of learning. The empty seat at the Hebrew *seder* is actually a question mark for table talk.

As has been said by Bacon, content makes man full, but "conversation makes a ready man." The social aspect of man, the need and "the will to communicate" (Jaspers) should be in view in "human-shaped education." The physical involves eating, helping, playing, and other common physical and social pleasures, which creates a familial environment and cherishes civility. This moves commercial enterprise ahead quite famously through enduring thoughts and endearing relationships.

There is no doubt that the three annual feasts of the Jewish year of eight days each, with physical and social elements in juxtaposition with the religious, preserved that remarkable people, in the midst of implacable enemies and inexorable adversity. That nation is the *Instructress of the World* through the Torah (Disraeli), with its saving Absolutes, an educational system of 3000 years' duration. It is no small example for those who desire their academies to endure.

The Spiritual and Moral

It is the spiritual and moral dimension of man that informs the heart and will of man to "cut-off evil at the pass" or "stand in the gap" for the land. There are no heroes without that. And even more important is the heroism of the diurnal – day-by-day embracing the TRUE, the GOOD, and the BEAUTIFUL. A person must derive values that transcend the present to be a full member of the race. Historicism is the modern literary idiocy, a heresy that limits all understanding of Truth to the present – truth with a very small "t". It is subjective – it's all about me. It is agreed by most that morals and ethics are beyond culture and above the individual, and they are informed and illuminated by history and literature, particularly the holy histories.

In *The Aims of Education* (1929), Alfred North Whitehead convincingly posits that education (particularly at the university) is religious. Loyalty and reverence should be the virtues of the truly educated. The history of education gives adequate testimony to this, because Jewish, Muslim, and Christian education, including most universities before this century, was founded for the purpose of spiritual nourishment and character formation. It is from these fountains that modern man has drunk the creative elixir for the arts, sciences and technology.

Robert Hutchins, in introducing *The Great Books of the Western World*, saw Western Civilization on the brink of the abyss if it did not return to her moral and spiritual moorings. He called for "The Great Conversation" with classical literature. Here we find moral ethical and spiritual content that recognized man as a responsible being. Tolstoy's "Anna Karenina" faced the consequences of her moral decisions. "Magnum, P.I.," may jump in bed with a stranger, usually female, or drink coffee and tea with the same amoral aplomb. Values are confined to the present existential act of consuming, whether persons or things. Protagoras said, "Man is the measure of all things." The measure of Post-Christian man is how much he can send, how many creative attachments he can forward so that what goes around will come around to the self-congratulating intellectual drone.

It must not be forgotten that both the context and content of the great literature and the arts, which have nurtured Western Civilization, have as the fountainhead the Judeo-Christian heritage and the Holy Scriptures. Remove it, and you will never find Raphael, Bach, or Shakespeare. However, there is a concomitant debt owed to the Greco-Roman confluence, which forms the mighty river (rather polluted at this point) known as Western Civilization.

Aesthetics, Creativity, and Imagination

Suppose some modern art were found 1000 years hence next to a Rembrandt, perhaps *Aristotle Contemplating a Bust of Homer*. The archaeologists would look at the former, a Dadaist "paint-dripping," and agree that they painted their homes rather sloppily at the turn of the twentieth century. The Rembrandt would combine creation and its forms with history, comparing understandably with other representations of the famous Greeks. In the light of nature and history, the true art would be identified.

True education must be a part of history and build upon it. Its mission is to transfer culture from one generation to the next. The imagination is the dynamic catalyst, which gives insight and passion to the truth of the culture. Aesthetics, the love of *kalos* (beauty and virtue), is nurtured in an atmosphere of freedom bounded by form. Form is understood through the created universe, and the subjective gift of imagination (the imaging of an expanding reality) is a response to what God has made as the Creator. Man as the *sub-creator* forms "new creations" from the given creation and the artifacts passed on through history in art, music, architecture, and literature in terms of natural forms. Is it possible that when man is alienated from *nature and nature's God* that he moves toward the vulgar and formlessness?

Udo Middleman of L'Abri, in a lecture on ownership and property, shows how a person who rents or lives in a welfare situation is stifled in his or her creativity. It is the property owner who naturally produces the most beauty in gardening and interior decorating. It is not money that makes the difference. Ownership gives a freedom to express creatively. Even citizens are actually aliens (fr. *alien,* lit, "without a lien or investment in"). For success in education, there should be an *ethos* of ownership in order to engender creativity, and thus beauty as the product of imagination. It is therefore the sacred duty of all who are involved with human-shaped education, from the kitchen table to the halls of academia, to provide ownership, form, and freedom; to teach the inescapable universals and absolutes, as well as the necessary particulars that are the means to the **True**, the **Good**, and the **Beautiful**.

Any worthwhile education should accommodate the whole man in his world and God's, otherwise it falls far short of what should be truly called "higher" education. Has anyone dared identify our present pedagogical scene as "lower" education?

CHAPTER 9

THE SIGNIFICANCE OF THE ARTS AND HUMANITIES FOR EDUCATION

Man needs more to think with than his brain! Socrates said in *Theaetetus* that "liberal education has free use of words and phrases rather than precision; the opposite is pedantic . . . do we perceive **with** our eyes and ears or **through** them?" When we speak of liberal education, we have in view the humanities, the arts, and the classics. Christian philosophy demands that the educational enterprise furnish the mind with a choice of good things, a smorgasbord of intellectual and aesthetic delights, which reflect a beautiful, orderly universe. It points to the fact of a moral structure to the universe which in turn strongly suggests an all-wise and moral Creator.

When we speak of liberal education, we have in view the humanities, the arts, and the classics. Christian philosophy demands that the educational enterprise furnish the mind with a choice of good things, a *smorgasbord* of intellectual and aesthetic delights. Like good wine, made better and more scintillating by time, the humanities and the arts are received by Western Civilization gratefully from the confluences of Greco-Roman and Judeo-Christian cultures. But the grateful are now diminished in numbers. There are all too few whose tastes have been properly developed in the legacy of literature and art. Neil Postman did not know that we would be "amusing ourselves to death" with our IPODS and *texting,* but it seems there is not time nor attention for developing a taste for the arts and the humanities.

In a gathering of business leaders at Princeton, Arch Davis IV, President of *The John Witherspoon Institute,* gave this report: "Leaders no longer prefer the professional computer programmers with B.S. degrees. It is too late to train them in language, critical thought, and human relations." The conferees agreed that **it was *more economical to hire liberal arts, humanities, history, and music majors.*** They can always provide on-the-job training for the personnel in the particular technological system, but *turning a machine into a person* at that stage of the commercial game is not practical.

Wonder of wonders! What seems impractical is practical, and what seems practical is impractical. *Persons* are needed. Francis Schaeffer pointed out the need of inter-disciplinary studies with these words:

> *Today we have a weakness in our educational process in failing to understand the natural associations between the disciplines. We tend to study all the disciplines in unrelated parallel lines... We have studied our exegesis as exegesis, our theology as theology, our philosophy as philosophy; we study*

> *music as music, not understanding that these things are of man, and the things of man are never unrelated parallel lines.*
>
> ### (Vol. I, Works, Escape from Reason, 211)

I would suggest that the reason why this weakness exists throughout both secular and religious institutions is an abysmal ignorance of the humanities and the arts. If one were cleverly putting down an opponent in a college debate and called him "Lilliputian," he would probably say, "Don't call me no girl!" If one were called a Cubist the retort might be, "Man, one thing I am not is a square!"

This is the day to answer the challenge of Francis Bacon for the liberal enterprise to create generalists. These are not those who claim to be "expert men [who] can execute and perhaps judge particulars one by one." He states positively that the "plotting and marshaling of affairs… come from [the] learned." The generalist, with sufficient knowledge correlated and absorbed, can make a cohesive whole in thought and expression. This is the province of liberal arts education.

The university should have *unity* and *diversity*, yet today it generally expresses one worldview – *the uniformity of natural causes in a closed system* (Schaeffer). Dividing itself into various departments without the *forum* for exchanging thought is mere *myopia*, not diversity. How may philosophy think of the ethical problems of the sciences without this? How may the moral dimension inform the political and scientific disciplines?

Higher education is practically disposed to *making a living* rather than *living the life* of **Truth, Goodness, and Beauty**. The true purpose of education is to assist man to become what he is in terms of his own history and culture through the humanities and the arts. To teach obedience to the Truth, living out life in the light of his learning, at any cost. Of course, training is also necessary through science, technology, and business savvy to produce and make a living.

Allan Bloom in *The Closing of the American Mind* (1986) said that most of the university curriculum is such training, and it can be done in two years. The rest of the time is mere filler. One may not agree with his assessment, but it may be mainly wands of cotton candy and fields of marshmallows at least sufficient to sweeten the undergraduate's future money. As has been noted earlier, corporations still have to train the graduates they get in their particular scheme of things. We would agree with Alfred North Whitehead's thesis that university education must develop loyalty and devotion. Today is the day of involvement without commitment, as the *mores* of marriage, university exams, Wall Street antics, and politics indicate.

What are the benefits of expanding the horizon of religious education beyond mere theological nomenclature and biblical data? Let us name but a few. In a foreword to *De Incarnatis* by Athanasius, C. S. Lewis shows that a classic spans cultures and generations, and contains the universals, *i.e., that which belongs to man as man, the triumph and tragedy of the human condition.* The classic endures the test of time, and can be read and enjoyed many times over and has a message from the springtime to the winter of life. The classics give a view of man that has moral absolutes, teaching natural and logical consequences in ethical choices. So long Tom Clancey, welcome Faulkner, Dickens and Dante.

Great art, music, and literature furnish the material for thought which reproduces more thought. The humanities develop imagination and creativity, much needed for powerful, informed rhetoric and enduring, persuasive writing. Reading great literature develops language skills through presenting the exemplars for good writing. Both music and art reflect the beauty of the form, color, and order of nature, and enlarge the souls of those who engage the senses in the joy of those arts.

The principal artifacts of a culture are the art, music, language, customs, literature, architecture, religion and science. **Therefore, the survival of a culture is totally dependent on the present generation receiving and passing on the "cultural DNA!" If there is nothing in your hand or brain, you have nothing to pass on!**

Spiritual and moral renewal in Western Civilization is dependent on the classics, especially sacred writings, which remain profoundly obscure. Without both the Old and New Testaments, the source of Judeo-Christian influence, a *neo-renaissance* will be as elusive as Eleusian mysteries. And as to the Greco-Roman confluence in the river of Western Civilization fed by the Hebrew and Christian tributaries, what would we do without Homer, Plato, Seneca, and Cicero? Nothing is more necessary for twenty-first century civilization than Greek justice for the person and Roman equity for property (all the *stuff* of civilization).

For the family, reading great books together and appreciation of the arts will teach the child to enjoy life, perhaps forever, and give a legacy for the children yet to be. The patent and passive experience of television leaves the mind of a person like the screen when it is turned off – nothing's there! The person has vanished! And as fast food, four televisions plus texting and twitter, iTunes and Facebook, is there time for mutual disquisition (intelligent social discourse)? No wonder politics is all images and shock radio and never a discussion of ideas.

What is more proper in the art of being human, including the *imago dei,* created in the image of God, than to enjoy life through that which is **Good, and True, and Beautiful?** And what is more boorish and boring than the *one-dimension man* who denies himself the vast parameters of the humanities, which are the very heart of "human-shaped education" and Western culture? A return to Socratic education is needed according to Allan Bloom at the end of his polemic "essay" as he calls his three-hundred plus pages. With the informal settings of walks and talks, questions and answers, and the child-like "show-and-tell" exchanges, love for the **Truth** is engendered. One theological student said that since being in a Socratic educational module, he had been moved to undertake the reading of Aristotle's **Politics** and Calvin' **Institutes**, a graduate student who completed college with little or no appreciation of reading anything but the Bible. Tutorials, table talk, and both reading and writing essays inevitably lead to an advancement in language and literature, as well as creativity, critical thought, and hunger for more knowledge in expanding areas.

I attended a renowned liberal arts college notable for its endowment, enduement, and its basketball team. I read its quarterly publication with great interest and enjoyment. But I have felt more and more that something was missing. The issue on the academic and professorial achievements of the school was beyond impressive. But there was no *beyondness.* There was not one reference to the Transcendent even in the Religion Department article. The psychology professor did speak of spirituality, which is perhaps a Gnostic ghost, with scarcely an upward glance.

The worldview was that of Protagoras who thought he had had it all: "Man is the measure of all things." If man begins with himself he will end with himself. That is outrageous loneliness in a vast universe that still has no room for the *noumena, **something from outside**.*

Socrates confessed both his ignorance and wonder at such profundity, and as he turned to leave, in what seemed an act of surrender, he paused and simply asked with upraised arm, "Did you say man is the measure of all things?" What man, Protagoras, you or I?" The sense of wonder has been lost and King *Academia* does not know that he has no clothes. Did not the great *nihilist* Sartre in his mellow years wishfully say, "What this world needs is an infinite reference point?" Socrates, that clever gnome, modeled the curmudgeon Columbo who used the same dialectic simplicity to get at the Truth.

History cogently informs us that the advancement of the church with those significant effects on society that had historical meaning was through the Christian Humanists with burning hearts and the Gospel. We need only think upon Patrick, Colomba, Luther (yes, Erasmus, too), Calvin, Wesley, Whitefield, Edwards, and Wilberforce to know this is so. Holy history, Joseph, Moses, Daniel, Nehemiah, and Paul were cultured and transcultural, fully engaged with culture and empires from Pharaoh to Caesar. Did they live and move in God or did God move and live in them? Clearly, you cannot have one without the other.

The Christian cannot be satisfied as long as any human activity is either opposed to Christianity or out of all connection with Christianity. It must pervade not only all nations, but also all of human thought. The Christian, therefore, cannot be indifferent to any branch of earnest Christian endeavor. It must all be brought into the same relation to the Gospel. It must be studied in order to be demonstrated as false, or else in order to be useful in advancing the Kingdom of God. The Kingdom must be advanced not only extensively but intensively.

THE CHURCH MUST SEEK TO CONQUER NOT MERELY EVERY MAN FOR CHRIST,
BUT ALSO THE WHOLE OF MAN.
J. Gresham Machen, ***Christianity and Culture***, 1912.

PART TWO

INCISIVE INSIGHTS –
COLLEGE OF FELLOWS, ICSI

CHAPTER 10

HUMANISM AND INHUMANE EDUCATION

Ann Oliver Iverson

★ This brief essay by Ann Oliver Iverson (1929-1995) was published by Institute of Christian Studies International (1988) and in republishing this monograph here we honor her dedicated life and service to the education in graduate schools, middle schools, church schools, the young, and especially her extended covenant family. If we updated to twenty-first century footnotes and statistics, it would be even more timely. It helps to know where we are by being reminded of where we have been. Things have changed, but not for the better. It is conspicuous in the twenty-first century that the research and data indicated are exponential, disturbing, and at times terrifying. Ann taught English Grammar at the International School of Theology to prepare first-year students, mostly engineering and business majors, for Greek 101. WTI

E. I. Rhone *wrote, "The human in humanism is missing. No system has more consistently and with such delicious aplomb proven to be antithetical to its name and purpose. It is a tragic joke." This monograph, written by an inner-city learning specialist who lived her life in the "City of Man," gives a brief overview of the implications of the humanist goals for education. With "man as the measure" the bar is too low for the education of a whole human being. The logical conclusion of modern education in the main yields a preponderance of straw heads and empty hearts, as well as impoverished souls. We are raising up a generation of moral pygmies. Let us seek the Source of Truth, Beauty, and Goodness, three markers of the upward call to transcendence.*

First of all, let me introduce you to the sacred writings of the sincere humanists, seeking the good of mankind. My purpose is to show that when man starts with himself he will end with himself. We must begin with the "constitution" of that sincere man-centered movement and let this philosophy lead us to its logical conclusions.

The 15th and final tenet of the Humanist Manifesto, written in 1933, states:

"We assert that humanism will
(a) Affirm life rather than deny it;
(b) Seek to elicit the possibilities of life, not flee from it; and
(c) Endeavor to establish the conditions of a satisfactory life for all, not merely a few . . ."

Let us briefly examine some of the fruits in education 54 years after the humanists "declared themselves" and clearly set forth their goals. Just one example of what the humanists' goals are was expressed by a Harvard professor in an address at a childhood education seminar in 1973: "Every child in America entering school at the age of five is mentally ill because he comes to school with certain allegiances toward our Founding Fathers, our elected officials, his parents, a belief in a supernatural Being, toward the sovereignty of this nation as a separate entity . . . It's up to you teachers to make all these sick children well by creating the international children of the future" (CWA Newsletter, July 1984). Many similar statements can be found in any issue of The Humanist magazine.

In colonial days the United States was thought to be the most literate nation on earth. The motivation for learning to read and for education in general was that one might become knowledgeable of the Bible and its truths. The turning point of this situation was signaled by the takeover of Harvard by the well-meaning Unitarians ("hard" and "soft" humanists) in 1805. What gradually followed was the changing of the educational base from a God-centered worldview to a man-centered worldview.

The cost of education has increased astronomically, 2600% from 1952 to the present – an increase greater even than medical care. In 1983 the cost of public elementary and secondary education was 141 billion dollars. Indeed, there seems to be no positive correlation between dollars spent and effective education. Statistics reported in Time magazine, May 9, 1984, indicated that there were 24 million functional illiterates in the United States, including 13% of all 17 year-olds, virtually all of whom have had from eight to twelve years of compulsory public schooling.

By contrast, Japan has 100% literacy. In 1984 there were forty-nine countries that had a higher literacy rate than the United States. Has it improved? This is since the rise of many kinds of "specialists" who supplement the classroom teacher in attempting to meet children's particular learning needs. I am one of these specialists, and am formerly a classroom teacher who was responsible for the total education of all the children in my class. I have to wonder about the system of which I was a "special" part.

Fast Forward: *What has happened since Orwell's tragic 1984? It seems that the United States is not even rated in some twenty-first century studies in literacy. After every conceivable government program has been devised, we have fallen far behind in mathematics languages and science. Students from* *around the world come to our universities only to go off with the honors or stay on with the best jobs.*

Achievement scores are still far lower than in 1957 when the launching of Sputnik caused us to look critically at our educational system. The National Conference on Excellence in Education, appointed by President Reagan, made public its report in April 1983, after an 18-month study, entitled "A Nation at Risk: The Imperative for Educational Reform," decried "a rising tide of mediocrity . . . If an unfriendly foreign power had attempted to impose on America the mediocre educational performance that exists today, we might well have viewed it as an act of war" (Newsweek, May 9, 1984, p. 62).

Gradually over the previous 20 years, the importance of history and the classics has diminished, and we have witnessed the elevation of such classes as Black History, Women's Rights, Sex Education, Marriage and the Family; important indeed and not to be neglected, but not basic. This type of course relates to "affective education", which is defined as "educational activities that focus on the development of skills in decision-making, problem-solving, interpersonal communication, and intrinsic motivation." Teachers became responsible for teaching self-worth, self-esteem, and self-expression. This can be learned as well in *Les Miserables.*

In modern society self-expression is an extreme intemperance, a license to "do your own thing" —just read the newspaper. We moderns deny social interest, which used to be encouraged. Perhaps the independent self can only produce ultimate chaos.

The side effects of this pendulum swing are these: less emphasis on cognitive development; a decrease in achievement; remedial classes spawned; and expensive pampering to special interest groups. When I was in college, remedial classes would have been a contradiction. In one study, of all math classes offered in four-year colleges and universities, one fourth were remedial (*Physics Today*). Now it is closer to one third. One has to question whether the mediocrity is by design. Blumenthal indicts the NEA as a Trojan horse in our educational system.

Os Guiness in *The Dust of Death* examines the philosophical base of humanism. He says that "optimistic humanism" especially prevailed in *academia*, but it lacked sufficient basis for the full range of humanness – it dwelt on man's aspirations without accounting for his aberrations, inevitably producing alienation. This gave rise to pessimistic humanism. Man has assumed the ultimate responsibility since God is declared dead, leading to despair. Nietzsche's *angst* was precisely this: Man is alone in the universe with no ultimate Truth to which he may relate.

When the humanist paints a picture of our humanistic educational scene today, he etches a grotesque surrealism on the canvas. He includes pernicious and pallid pastels that are seductive. I have painted a severe landscape with grays and dark clouds in the background. The truth is that humanism is a contradiction in terms. It actually de-humanizes persons. While the claim is that it fosters life, humanists have brought death to education. The school-based clinics in our schools, under the guise of health and wellness, promote contraception and abortion. Values clarification encourages young people to cast off traditional mores for "do-it-yourself" ethics. Tenet Fifteen of the *Manifesto* states that "all, not just a few, shall have satisfactory lives," yet fewer succeed, and the increase of teen suicides dispels claims of the success of that goal.

By asserting that man is the measure of all things, we have lost our biblical moorings. Nietzsche, Camus and Dostoevsky agree that totalitarianism is not just a possibility, but the inevitable result of man's being in ultimate charge of the universe. Schools in the urban East have armed security guards and systems; many appear as minimum-security prisons.

The Reformation recovered not only doctrine and the Gospel, but the particular doctrine of Christian vocation. It is possible that many are being called to this magnificent opportunity to affect society for righteousness and for God, but have not the courage to answer. The one-dimensional Christian, seeking peace, security, and affluence, as Francis Schaeffer points out, is deafened to such a sense of calling. We ask, how may such men and women be nurtured for such a time as this?

The Christian educator has the Truth, which sets men free, and allows children to stay free. May that Truth be incarnate again in the people of God who will make strong commitments to tell the Truth, to live the Truth, and if need be, die for the Truth! Elton Trueblood said it best:

> *Christians have no monopoly on commitment; they simply have a different object. A Christian is a person who confesses that, amidst the manifold and confusing voices heard in the*

world, there is one Voice which supremely wins his full assent, uniting all his powers, intellectual and emotional, into a single pattern of self-giving. That voice is Jesus Christ . . . he believes in him with all his heart and strength and mind. Christ appears to the Christian as the one stable fulcrum in all the relativities of history. Once the Christian has made this primary commitment, he still has perplexities, but be begins to know the joy of being used for a mighty purpose by which his little life is dignified. (Lecture Notes, Hereford Conference, 1984)

<u>Note:</u> **This essay is as timely for the "post" postmodern world of the twenty-first century as it was in the last generation. In the light of this critique, only fools are not terrified.**

+++You may update the facts but the Truth remains+++

CHAPTER 11

MODELING AND MENTORING –
RICHARD SANNER
ENHANCING WHAT IS TAUGHT
THROUGH WHAT IS CAUGHT

It is well known that modern educators make the lecture the main method of teaching. Therefore, to even speak of content, both taught and caught, in the same breath would label one suspect in some educational circles. In the direct, content-laden pedagogy, the teacher and his activity as a lecturer are depended upon to carry the content to the learner. As effective as this method may be at times, it is inadequate by itself to impart a lifestyle of moral and spiritual character that certain information demands.

It is a necessity for those teaching theology to incorporate modeling and mentoring to demonstrate and enhance what they teach. The very fact that the Scriptures speak of life transformation as the goal for learning makes the transmissive (lecture) educational method inadequate. To give meaningful insight into life through a lecture is one thing, but to live out that insight in a context outside of the classroom in different educational contexts, and over a period of time, is quite another. The living out of life for a period of time with students is a goal of the teacher who wants to aid the student in preparing to live out content in life's context, making the Truth incarnate.

Our Lord's example strongly suggests that the discipling form of education with some lecturing is the best way to impart most theological knowledge. Perhaps this is because the nature of biblical revelation is "alive and active;" that at appropriate points the truths of Scripture are better taught, understood, and applied through this method. This will put greater burden upon the teacher, for he or she will have to be far more transparent and creative in the teaching process as a whole. It demands vulnerability, which is, for some, a severe dying. Keeping this in mind, let us proceed to outline several key aspects of this type of education.

First, it is important to distinguish between the two concepts of taught and caught. This is not easy, for there is an overlap at points. But to help in making the distinction I will draw upon the incisive comments made by Dr. Wayne Rood in his educational classic, *The Art of Teaching Christianity* (1977). Dr. Rood uses the terms "knowledge about", which I will equate with the idea of "taught" and "knowledge of" which I will equate with the idea of "caught". He states:

> "Knowledge about" is achieved directly by observation and refined through its deductive consequences, but it never knows the inside, the actual nature of things. It is knowledge about things, physical events, and moral

behavior from the outside. It is satisfactorily reducible to objective assertions of fact, and this is one of the tests of truth. It is of the nature of the objective world, other than the knower, implacable, unaffected by wish. It is hard-nosed, universally true if true at all. It is observable, measurable, manipulatable, dealing with information, data, statistics, labels resulting in theory and description. It is the sort of knowledge on which science and its wonders are built. (Rood, 1977; p. 17).

On the other hand he defines "knowledge of" in the following manner: "It is direct in nature and achieved indirectly by association. Its content is immediately experienced, emotionally felt, and usually non-verbally expressed. It is of the nature of flesh-and-blood, but not merely of the self. It is knowledge of how things feel on the inside rather than about how they appear on the outside, knowledge of every *thing* as identified with one's self, but not merely subjective. It is individual, singular, profound, and secretive, but not merely subconscious. It is spiritual and intuitive, but not merely otherworldly or aesthetic. It deals with attitudes, convictions, and emotions and results in decision and action. It is the sort of knowledge from which art and its mysteries emerge (Rood, 1977; p. 16).

Thus in summary, we have two approaches to knowledge through two methods of teaching. Perhaps the strength of the transmissive (lecture) method is that it can give "knowledge about" a subject in a clear, concise way, drawing upon research in the field. On the other hand, "knowledge of" a subject can best be enabled through a modeling and mentoring approach outside the typical classroom and over a period of time.

I would agree with Dr. Rood that "about" and "of" are not mutually exclusive in nature. The educational experience cannot be complete unless teachers and students learn to value both. However, because Scriptures give us strong precedent to pursue, with intelligent implementation, the direct and experiential approach, many more of us teaching in seminaries and Bible colleges need to be actively engaged in this method. Jesus' disciples were the active participants in their own educational process, and became the first-century world change agents. In the same manner, students of the

Scriptures today need to be afforded such an opportunity, if they are to be transformed and transformers in the so-called postmodern era.

We insert the chart below from Mortimer Adler's description of true education—information (content by books, audio or lecture); experienced training, doing (*praxis*), and critical thought—the *maieutikos* midwifery of Socrates. Adler is indeed an authority being an editor of the *Oxford English Dictionary* as well as *The Great Books of the Western World*. Some education is only one thing—content; some is only practical training; without the maieutics education is aborted; and there is no critical thought without information and experience. It will be referred to again in terms of theological education in the Appendix.

Modeling, Mentoring and Knowing God

Modeling is the first step in this discipleship approach, and the teacher must accept this as a primary responsibility. The model is a person considered worthy of imitation and a source of inspiration, leading others to exemplary thinking and behavior. The goal would be to model the same qualities that Christ did, and be governed by the principles that governed Him. The major concern of modeling is that of allowing the student to participate with the teacher in the normal settings of life.

Mentoring is also a commitment to extra and longer-term involvement with the student. Whereas modeling focuses primarily upon the teacher and how he lives out the demands of Scripture, mentoring has its concern with the character formation of the student as he learns the content. The mentor is a close, trusted and experienced counselor or guide—and he is a friend. He must be objective enough to assess where a student is and then help to take him further toward accomplishing at least two very important goals. First are the personal goals of the individual, and secondly, is the stated purpose of the educational curriculum. There is a commitment to both, of course, but in that order.

Keeping in mind the modeling and mentoring aspects of education, there are several means by which this approach can be accomplished. For example, another professor and I taught Old Testament Survey and Evangelism as tandem classes. Each class met on different days of the week, one in my home, and the other in a church lounge. By virtue of the fact that both classes were constantly before us, the content of each was at points integrated or discussed freely in either class. In the survey class, the God of Abraham was viewed as a missionary God. Through His chosen people, beginning with Abraham, He would bring blessings (including salvation) to the nations of the world. This is integration. Thus, through the study of the Old Testament, a basis was established for evangelism, which enabled a broader perspective in the evangelism class.

But this is not all. Modeling began when the professors took at least an hour out of almost every class day, going out with the students witnessing in the community. Over a period of time, mentoring developed as students were evaluated (professors were evaluated too!) as to their abilities to think clearly about the implications of their learning in both classes. Communication of the gospel made them participants in relating and integrating the cognitive learning ("knowledge about") with the affective ("knowledge of"). The unmistakable result of this approach is the enhancement of what is taught by what is caught. "Knowledge of" helps the student to absorb at a deeper cognitive level than "knowledge about".

THE MAIEUTIC NECESSITY IN THE EDUCATIONAL PROCESS*
Mortimer Adler, *Paideia*

	LEAD BY TELLING	HOW TO DO	DOING IT
GOALS	ACQUISITION OF ORGANIZED KNOWLEDGE	DEVELOPMENT OF INTELLECTUAL SKILLS -SKILLS OF LEARNING	ENLARGED UNDERSTANDING OF IDEAS AND VALUES
MEANS	By means of DIDACTIC INSTRUCTION, LECTURES AND RESPONSESTEXT BOOKS AND OTHER AIDS	By means of COACHING, EXCERCISES AND SUPERVISED PRACTICE	By means of MAIEUTIC OR SOCRATIC QUESTIONING AND ACTIVE PARTICIPATION
AREAS, OPERATIONS AND ACTIVITIES	In three areas of subject matter LANGUAGE, LITERATURE, AND THE FINE ARTS MATHEMATICS AND NATURAL SCIENCE HISTORY, GEOGRAPHY, AND SOCIAL STUDIES	In the operations of READING, WRITING, SPEAKING, LISTENING CALCULATING, PROBLEM-SOLVING, OBSERVING, MEASURING, ESTIMATING EXCERCISING CRITICAL JUDGMENT	In the DISCUSSION OF BOOKS (NOT TEXTBOOKS) AND OTHER WORKS OF ART AND INVOLVEMENT IN ARTISTIC ACTIVITIES (e.g. MUSIC, DRAMA, VISUAL ARTS)

*The three columns are descriptive but not sequential. The educational process is a constant interplay of the cognitive, affective, and maieutic.

There was yet another step that was taken to make this approach educationally sound. We decided to take the class on a two-day retreat to a location where the results of the Fall of Man in Genesis could be seen vividly, and the need for the passion of our Lord Jesus Christ could be tested in their own hearts. Dr. Bill Iverson suggested our class go to the Union Rescue Mission in Los Angeles to serve tables and spend the night. We walked the streets and talked to the alcoholics and drug abusers, inviting them to a meal at the Mission. We preached in the city park and did dramatic biblical scenarios to illustrate the passion and power of the Lord.

Here the need for a larger spiritual perspective—a biblical one—began to be caught. It was found that some students had very little tolerance for the dirt of the city and of the people. On these facts alone it was enough to excuse themselves from a compassionate attitude. But the mentors encouraged biblical attitudes and convictions that we had been learning through our Bible Survey class. By helping our students be directly involved at the emotional level as well as the cognitive level, these conspired to force the will to move in the direction of life-changing decisions and taking appropriate action. "Those that know their God stand firm and take action."

The students will not soon forget the sensory impression of the Fall of Man in what they saw in the eyes of the homeless; smelled of the grime and the alcohol; heard in the sad stories of the transient; and touched when they helped the helpless to a meal. Just as Jesus was moved with compassion when He saw the multitudes "because they were distressed and downcast like sheep without a shepherd," so we too, teacher and student, could catch the significance of the Fall and be renewed in compassion for people in the midst of life.

They looked for a Shepherd who should "go before them"—that's modeling! . . . And who "called them by name . . . and they knew His voice and followed Him"—that's mentoring. **And who was "Mentor?"** *He was the wise Vice-Regent of Ulysses, entrusted with the stewardship of raising his son Telemachus to be a King. It was a twenty-year vocation. Thus mentors are charged to raise up a royalty of heart and head and hand, the highest calling of the human spirit.*

CHAPTER 12

TOOLS OF EDUCATION, OLD AND NEW

The Irenic Art of Elenchus – Richard Pensiero

*M*aieutics in real life! Mr. Pensiero is a philologist, bibliophile, a researcher, *and a very contrary man. His short essay makes the point historically regarding eristics – the art of tough-minded dialog. He also has a greasy computer because he is an automobile mechanic by trade. He is good at tuning brains and Buicks.*

We have been shown that the maieutic method is good, but we must understand that it is tough. Let us see how the way of Socrates has its rocks and pillows. **But first**, why do Perry Mason in court and Columbo in his "ignorant" questioning create such high drama? Why have *The Dialogues of Plato* continued as the most fascinating of ancient literature? A strong reason is *Elenchus!*

Elenchus was developed in the Eleatic School in the Greek colony of Elea in Sicily in the fifth century. It means cross-examination, and the Eleatic founders, Xenophanes and Parmenides, developed the *Law of Contradiction* and principles of logic making, this adamant art a weapon for intellectual warfare. It was popularized by Zeno, who lectured to 2000 students at times.

It was an irenic (*Gr. erene,* "peace") approach with Socrates because it was where mercy and truth met together. He was gentle with most, but ruthless with the pseudo-sophisticates. Plato further developed this in his writing. It is heuristic (discovery) learning, a joint inquiry leading to self-instruction. The genius of it is that the teacher leads (*educere*) rather than directs (*inculcere*); he replies rather than defends; he responds rather than reacts. It is true education.

Learning is not a passive experience; rather it requires an active and cooperative participation for the understanding that will weave itself into the fabric of daily living. The art of dialog provides a method of mutual investigation that allows for the import of conviction as well as knowledge. This often results in a positive change in behavior.

People are not persuaded to change their way of life by the reception of seemly and rational statements designed to appeal to the reason or emotion. Reciprocity in learning, the way of maieutic *elenchus,* committed to honesty and mutual respect, enhances for each learner internal persuasion, rather than impositions from another.

In discovering what is true about opinions, one must first ask questions about presuppositions and resolutely search out the implications for life as one lives it. As Socrates said, "The unexamined life is not worth living." The more one is open to maieutic questioning, the more new implications conflict with the original statement. A choice must be made. Welcome a change in the opinion because the original idea lacks warrant, and the search is expanded to find the truth that will stand up to the question. To reaffirm the original opinion, one must candidly concede that there is an inconsistency. This also leads to further searching. But I do not have to search far for easy listening. I can get in my Chevvy, pop a CD into the system, and hear Professor Ashworth's last class or Os Guiness in his famous *Dust of Death* lecture. My professor, Dick Sanner, explains it and my colleague Mel tells how a long commute can be a free education except for the gas pump. Our Core Module reached beyond books and class lectures.

Today as a lay teacher of worldviews and using maieutic ways, my students have iphones, ipods. ipads, itunes, You Tube and beyond, but my thesis stands: Technology is insufficient. A student and a gadget won't do.

Give me dialog or give me death! That is true educational liberty known as *liberal education*.

The Tutorial and the Essay – W. T. Iverson

*The academic part of mentoring and discipling is the **tutorial**, and a principal tool is the essay. The former comes from a word that means to guard (L. tutela; Fr. tueri, to look at); the latter word was coined by the greatest of essayists, Montaigne, meaning to make an attempt (Fr. essais). The tutor then is charged with the duty of protecting the total person, body, mind and soul. He is forever the **parentis in loci**. Liberal education and the university enterprise in general are failing for lack of the mentor and the discipline of the essay. This is not always intentional, for it may be caused by the institutional life and death struggle with numbers and economics. The explicit tools for an exact education of the grammarian together with romantic imagination, thus satisfying the poet, is the felicitous wedding of the tutorial and the essay. The fruit of this union is true education.* E. I. Rhone, ICSI Colleague

The tutor is teaching a person not just a subject. This relationship is very personal, usually one-on-one. The child was often made over in the image of the tutor, not that of the parents. The implications for this are ominous when we find that the personable humanist is all too often

131

the ward of our children. Sometimes he or she is more of a "inhumanist" according to Ann Iverson.

Good education must have the tutorials, which may be with one pupil or a very few. What is possible in either case is to deal with particulars in depth and to enable the forming of thoughts into generalizations, by which the student may become discretionary in dealing with ideas and life itself **on his own.** He is moved from a *dependent* thinker to an *independent* one, and with others becomes a colleague, or *inter-dependent.* This is the actual process of child rearing and is the very heart of the historic British system of education. The fruit of it, the tutorial-driven pedagogy, is apparent to those who would compare the parsimony of American education with the richness of the European.

On this point I asked Harry Blamires, the famous literary student of C. S. Lewis, what was the most significant learning experience with his mentor? He was quick to say that it was sitting on the floor with tea in his professor's home reading essays with other students. Into the tutorial the student brings his essay. The *informal* essay is a relatively short literary composition, dealing with one topic, often involving a good-natured attempt to persuade the reader. Plutarch and Cicero were essayists and didn't know it, while Francis Bacon (1580) joined his French contemporary, Montaigne, in making the essay an art form. The personal, conversational, relaxed and often humorous essay (Mark Twain, Charles Lamb) communicates thought in a negotiable form for all sorts and stations of people. It reveals the heart and mind together to a student, enabling him to develop the *right* side of his brain, *i.e.,* imagination, with a growing vocabulary and viable syntax for the rational man.

The *formal* essay is useful, and is more academic, with Matthew Arnold, Addison, and John Stuart Mill as good examples. It is more dogmatic, systematic, and expository. It is a good discipline for the *left* side of the brain. Without the tutorial and the essay, education reform on the secondary and university level is improbable, if not impossible. In applied studies in psychology, sociology, criminal justice, and theology, teachers need to utilize the informal essay. In the cluster colleges and the university, it will generally involve the hybrid essay, which allows for both solid data and heart expression.

The matriculating term, **tuition,** is derived from *tutela,* and has come to mean what someone has paid for their education. One wonders how lectures, often by untested graduate students to two hundred impoverished freshmen, beginning with heads of straw and hollow chests, could possibly fulfill the financial contract of the institution. Plato's *Academe* had the happy admixture of lecture and dialog, for Socratic philosophers were welcome anytime. Such education met the expectations for the investment made by the nobility of Athens for their youth.

> *We salute the mentors who model and the mentoring tutors who form whole persons to "out-think, out-live, and out-die" this generation.*

Core Module Education – Richard Sanner

Concept: How to help the busy person capture learning time through listening to Sproul and again to my lectures on the freeway, followed by a class at Denny's in San Bernardino. The busy person can slice his time through media – education as a lifestyle.

Imagine the business person, busy at least forty hours a week with a job; then family, friends and all the extracurricular activities sandwiched in between—it's like another thousand jobs. And then there is the commitment to God and His work. Heavy on the mind is what to do and how to do it. With all the talents, abilities, training and experience, is it enough to just sit in the pew on Sunday morning? Is this fulfilling one's commitment to God? No, probably not. But what may one do about it?

The use of media in the core module educational approach may be the answer. It may help that busy person take advantage of those slices of time to learn, and when appropriate, put all of those God-given talents to use in a fulfilling ministry. There are no prerequisites other than a strong desire to grow in the knowledge of God and His revelation to us, and to use that knowledge to advance the cause of Christ.

How then might a busy person be served in this type of opportunity? For example, almost all of the courses used in core module education in varied educational programs are on CD's or on line so that listening in the car to a lecture by a top scholar is a cinch. Many lectures and classes are on videos and such notables as Ravi Zacharias are on You Tube, but watching as one drives has its limitations. We suggest that our students listen to a lecture at least twice, once for reflection and thinking, and another time to actually take notes. . Again, the latter cannot be done while driving unless one is adept at looking, listening, learning, thinking and writing all at the same time! One must always create a good study place for listening, reading, and writing to attain excellence in learning.

After having learned from an audio lecture, we get together in a core module type of setting to discuss the significance of what was learned. This is done in a small group fashion about once a week for six weeks, or bimonthly for twelve weeks. Yes, these meetings take a little extra time, but it is worth it. In this setting the busy person comes alive as mind and heart are challenged together. We might even ask this busy person to do a little writing – just a little, mind you (which is really not too painful) – and the outcome is often very surprising. Then the inevitable happens – he writes more than ever asked for, and loves it!

For example, after having gone through a short exercise like writing an essay, the busy person finds there is a greater sense of conviction in his life and the Bible takes on greater importance in the rest of the pressing aspects of life. Some of the busyness may seem to diminish and even disappear as priorities are evaluated and changed. Time is more precious than money.

There are many benefits to using media as an approach to help the busy person get more meaning out one's daily life. It is also a good approach for the person who has more margins of leisure such as those retired, or with children out of the nest. The more a person learns in those brief slices of time in life, the more he or she will be able to give back to God and to others. Think about it! You can be a pioneer in the inner space of your own heart and mind with media input and core module education! Let Mel Folkerstsma, a Core Module Mentor who paid his dues, explain further.

Between Walden and the Whirlwind—Mel Folkerstsma

How can a man with a mortgage, wife, three kids, and a job working rotating shifts get into theological education? How can he participate in class on the Christian life?

Perhaps the dilemma of the workingman and his education must take a novel approach. Well, not really as novel as you think. Only in recent times has formal education been confined to structured schedules and ivy-covered walls. Look at the example of Jesus. Rabbi is the Hebrew title given to Him as a Master-teacher, but He never had a classroom. The typical school of His day was similar to the early Greek education as practiced by Socrates. This consisted of men conversing beside an amphitheater or while walking to the marketplace.

Jesus could have successfully opened a school by the Jordan River, kept hours, and screened GPA's and grant forms for potential applicants; but He chose instead to offer His knowledge to any and all who would listen, never excluding anyone hungry for the truth. He was always available, and class was always in session. It was the type of classroom that started with God asking Adam an obvious question, "Where are you, Man?" Today we have become accustomed to conferred degrees, air-conditioning, power point, and the lecturing professor. The school is denoted as a campus even as the church has become a building. Given the practicality of learning in life situations, one wonders if education has evolved or devolved.

One premise for education is that no person who wants to grow in the knowledge of truth should be prohibited from doing so, and be penalized for his limiting circumstances. It may be inconvenient for the teacher, but time is of essence – perhaps the dedicated mentor would have a breakfast class for the night-shift worker. I have seen the model in my teachers. Let me share a little of my experience.

I recall nights at the "Pizza Chalet," a church basement, or a living room. Days found us at "Dudley's Sandwich Shop," "Royale Restaurant," or somewhere in-between. Every class was a potential field trip – Yucaipa Regional Park, purportedly for laid-back fishing, turned out to be a five-hour marathon class. It would have been a shorter session but it's hard to make points when the fish are biting. The students could not understand why the teacher, Dick Sanner, was catching the most fish. Was it prosperity doctrine? I insist that it was Providence.

One class began at "Dudley's" and ended at "Burger King." On the way from one to the other, we were assigned to go to a public place and ask, "What is a Christian?" Everyone was late, because the question opened the door to some Gospel answers. I remember the helpful UPS driver whose response was; "You need to go to Mission Aviation if you want to find out. Those people know about that stuff!"

One of the great rewards of this process is that the intellect is stimulated, and thinking replaces stuffing. Periods of silence allowed for interruptions, as questions were elevated and erring answers redirected; more searching elicited more and wiser questions. It was at times like the *elenchus* of the Eleatic School of ancient philosophy. Formative faith often began to emerge which would ultimately affect personal conduct and biblical worldview. What I have been describing is Core Module Education. It is not some sort of convenience store learning. It drives student and mentor from their pious comfort zones, and enhances holistic growth for all. Perhaps you would like to risk it.

And remember . . . Not only is "the unexamined life not worth living" but "The unlived life is not worth examining." Quotes from Socrates and E. I. Rhone.

PART THREE

THE COMMUNITY: WHERE FACTS AND FORMATION MEET THE TRUTH

We see in Jesus the Hebrew model of loving God, which is none other than expressing love through teaching – while walking, talking, eating, rising and retiring, in the marketplace and by the city gate. The dialogue goes on informally. School is never out, for it is in all of life, at all times and places, sacred and profane, at the dinner table or conference table, in a planned peripatetic experience in the city, or a walk, arm in arm, on a lovely river trail. It may include the exacting dialectic, adducing knowledge, or a maieutic experience, giving birth to self-knowledge. It is the early Greek model of Socrates rather than the scholastic model of the later Plato of the Academy and his student, Aristotle.

The question: Can this be transferred into theological educational systems today, given the human element of inertia and the practical problem of financial survival in the institution—the more students the more income? The writer sees this as a contest between economics, tradition, and inert bureaucracy with the explicit demands made by man's nature and the implicit demands made by the example of the Master Teacher.

The Idea of a Study Center *as an historic essay is by no means worthy of the Schaeffer family to whom it is dedicated. But as I think of Francis, Edith, Priscilla, Susan, Debbie and Franky, I pray that the Lord of the Fragments will take that which is scattered across the world and gather it up into His arms and bless it again. May He send forth the influence of this family in word and deed to the ends of the earth, till He comes to say, "Well done, My good and faithful servant. Enter into the joy of the Lord." The second essay was inspired by the Bronx Household of Faith in the heart of the city as well as Al Santino, one of my students who later founded a study center. May God raise up many more who will be vulnerable, humble servants, committing body and soul to spiritual formation in the hearts and minds of all who seek.*

CHAPTER 13

THE IDEA OF A STUDY CENTER

A Human-Shaped History of Education

*A*n essay is a humble thing. Although the famous essayists seem to be vast egotists, it is not really so. Rather they are egoists, secure enough in the centrality of their persons to venture an idea which they truly own. It is encouraging indeed that an essay is a mere attempt, and that is my comfort here. The essayist may not claim he has the answer, but he is convinced enough to center on one idea, and, except for the apologist and politico, he would gently persuade his reader. With a liberating confidence in the **idea** and with Socratic ataraxy, he keeps a cool head and is disabused as to whether he "wins" or not. I therefore call on this time-honored means of communication to present a neglected aspect of education.

   Perhaps I should be ashamed to confess it, but I do write with a hot hand. I am persuaded that the subject before us has to do with one aspect of education (defined by E. I. Rhone as simply the passing of culture from one generation to the next) without which the sad demise of Western civilization is inevitable. It is on the edge of the abyss, to use the strong language of Robert Hutchins introducing the "Great Books of the Western World." Persons such as Charles Malik, Allan Bloom, Mortimer Adler and Chancellor Hutchins have written on the state of education with hand and heart fully engaged in identifying a Post-Western World. I warn the reader that I seek to persuade through lessons from history as well as from common observations of ourselves and our contemporaries.

A Short History of Education in Western Civilization

Let us first call on historical witnesses in the commendation of the small academy. John Henry Newman's famous essay on the *The Idea of the University* offers much that is salvific to our modern educational quandary. His idea of the university was vastly different from ours in that we mainly think of large-scale training and economic enterprises, research, and government grants. He was thinking of "the ancient method – **the living man and the living voice.**" He was thinking of the art of living and character; we all too often think of making a living and existing. We think of departments, each a kingdom; he was speaking of colleges (colleagues, "bound together by common goals"), forming the university. We are looking for technique and "how to's"; Cardinal Newman was thinking of "whys." He was not thinking of rationalism, but the rational. To him, humanism, measuring all things without a dimension outside of Man, would diminish the human. He makes his case for the humanity and urbanity of true education.

Although Newman wrote over 150 years ago, he observed that there were books, papers, tracts enough on every corner "in great exuberance." "Yet", he said, "we must repair to the teacher of wisdom to learn wisdom." He spoke of the university as unity in diversity. For the *studium general,* strangers must come from every corner of the world, sharing their diverse knowledge in mutual learning.

Newman also considered the city as the true university. Where better to learn politics than at Parliament, readily available to the student? Where may one best learn engineering than in works of Sir Christopher Wren – cathedrals, public buildings, and bridges – all exquisite and structurally sound, enduring yet aesthetically approaching perfection? Where would one learn of the arts but in the theaters and museums of the city? Where would one learn best to serve in religious matters but in the varied churches and ministries of the city?

Although all such institutions need not be in the city, the city should be in the institutions. Study centers and small cluster colleges should consciously seek to be in the *polis*, unless there are other circumstances related to their history and mission that would direct otherwise. Newman is careful to point out, however, that if the university is in the city, the country must be in the university. He cited the University of Paris on the left bank of the Seine, occupying almost half of Paris at one time, with multiplied gardens and a verdant landscape. Without the beauty of nature, education would be a drab affair, and would ultimately destroy creativity and initiative through aesthetic starvation.

Socrates and Jesus were much in the world and saw that education was a lifestyle. School was never out, but was for anybody, anywhere, at anytime. Even before Socrates was executed for seeking to change the political structure through the Truth and the moral (spiritual) education of youths on the streets and in the *agora,* his student Plato had a vision. He would give the rest of his life to *the academy.* He had hoped that his academy would send true citizens of courage and virtue into the society of Athens or give their very lives at a Thermopolis – to make a difference for the Republic. In spite of the turbulence of Greek history, Plato's "university" lasted 900 years.

Students found many styles of learning in Athens: Epicurus reclining among bowers of flowers, a perpetual picnic and garden party; Zeno conversing on his portico; and Aristotle, the peripatetic teacher, "walked the legs off of his students," as Newman points out. A foremost example of a student in Athens would be Marcus Aurelius. A most enlightened

Emperor of Rome and a Stoic philosopher, he came to study Zeno. But equally impressive as we move from prince to peasant, there is Cleanthes, the boxer, centuries earlier. He hauled water and did servile things to pay his tutor, the high-minded Zeno. He ultimately became head of the Stoic school at the death of the master Stoic.

Although the personal was central in the Greek academy, we should know that there were also popular teachers such as Theophrastus, who attracted 2000 students from all parts of the world. He lectured necessarily as the Sophist must, but he had disciples as the key to his teaching and learning. We still need great lecturers, but a culture will die without the urbane disciple-teacher. Mentoring creates moral leaders, given moral mentors.

The reader knows that Homer wrote his epic poetry regarding events of perhaps 1100 B.C. some three centuries later. The themes were courage, loyalty, and submission to the will of the gods. There was a "Middle Age of Chivalry," knights and all, followed by a Dark Age, strangely like Europe fifteen centuries later, a reversed order in history. Suddenly, bursting upon the history of Western culture are luminaries still unparalleled in intellectual history – Thales, Pericles, Demosthenes, Sophocles, Aeschylus, Xenophanes, Isocrates, Socrates, Plato, and Aristotle. Poetry, architecture, arts, medicine, and democracy flourished. I would like to think these yet nurture our minds and souls in the present century. I also wonder if social scientists today like Jeremy Rifkin are not right in replacing Social Darwinism with Social Entropy. Really, have we improved at all since that day in Greece or is it a downward spiral, except for technology?

We realize that there are times for cultures to grow, withdraw, return, and decline, as Toynbee illustrates. Climate, location, exploration, scientific discoveries, trade, political and military events all conspire to bring about history. Add to this men and women with ideas and courage to test those ideas existentially, and history is created. Everything else is mere chronology. Greece was the right place at the right time with the right people. Greece today is a sad affirmation that entropy is inexorable.

Newman's vision for his beloved Oxford, where he spent thirty years, was that it be "the fountainhead of Christianity, students flocking from East, West, South and North; from America, Australia, Egypt and India, with the ease and rapidity of locomotion *not yet discovered.*" What a surprise he would have if he knew how rapidly a student might now come to Oxford from India! But not all are able to come. Could not the small *collegium,* the study center, be developed in distant lands and cities, using the technology of travel, books, and electronics to provide the lecturers and information? And would not the very nature of man, given the context, produce relevant moral and spiritual learning in any land? Yes it could, if there were *in loci* that midwife through whom mercy and truth meet together. The nature of the man-child demands assistance at birth.

I would like to propose that it was human-shaped education that made the difference in Greece, and at the heart of it was *Socratic midwifery* or **MAIEUTICS** *(Gr. maieutikos,* lit., "of midwifery"). In the first half of the twentieth century, Dewey called for the Socratic examination, and his followers scholasticized his ideas into social engineering programs, with B. F. Skinner becoming the high priest. Allan Bloom, on the last page of his compelling essay, calls for Socratic inquiry to return to the university again. This leads us to related questions as to the best methods of pedagogy, and in what environment may young minds best be nurtured?

Pedagogy is defined as teaching method and its principles. For the education of children today, pedagogy means a variety of media and lots of activity. But even more sadly, with adults, learning is generally confined to the lecture trap or programmed learning – automotons spoonfed with facts.To use Margaret Mead's terms, it is *vertical transmission* rather than *lateral transmission.* Kierkegaard said that the lecture pedagogy was the poorest, and today educational researchers generally agree that it is the least effective method.

Let us adopt the term and practice of *androgogy* (Gr. lit. "leading man") to inform our modern pedagogy (lit. "leading children"). *Androgogy* is teaching women as women and men as men, not as mere children. The person is not John Locke's *tabula rasa* with blanks to fill in, but a person with an inherent sense as to what is the **True**, the **Good**, and the **Beautiful**. It is that dialogical endeavor that turns facts into knowledge and thus is truly possessed by the learner. If this knowledge is essential, existential truth, it will also possess the learner. The androgogical process of education necessitates security, identity, and integrity on the part of the teacher and creates these in the learner; it allows her or him to risk the dialogue, and to seek to find the other person as she or he is.

Matthew Arnold contrasted Socrates' manner of communication with that of Pericles, the golden-tongued orator. The latter was, perhaps, the greatest speaker in history, but his admiring auditors went away forgetting what he said. With Socrates, however, "the point would stick fast in the mind and one cannot get rid of it." Research demonstrates that the lecture method in its overuse creates "passive accepters of the opinions of others" rather than active thinkers in their own right. T. F. Stoval shows that learning, recall, and application are significantly higher in discussion as compared to the lecture method. True dialogue is not the pooling of ignorance, but a community of minds sharing what each has to offer, with mutual corroboration leading to more truth or even **The Truth.**

Jacob Comenius, the father of historic Reformation education, said it this way:

> *To ask many questions, to retain the answers,*
> *And to teach what one retains to others;*
> *These enable the student to surpass his master.*

What happens with the maieutic process is the eliciting from the other person what he thinks and who he perceives himself to be, in order that he may *know what he truly knows and who he really is.* It also vacates false ideas and creates more space for learning content. Socrates helped his colleagues to lay "wind eggs" in order to disabuse them as to their vaunted knowledge. *Education* in the Latin literally means "leading out from." It is that more perspicuous view of education which consists in the drawing out of what is in the pupil rather than cramming into him a mass of material from without. Is it possible that our youth today are not being so truly educated, as were the youth in the schools of Socrates, Plato, and Aristotle?

It is only in this human approach to education that there are moral, ethical, and spiritual dimensions which, if excluded, doom the process to failure. The culture is thus empty of meaning, and its days are numbered. It is in humane way-of-life learning that character is built. Lamentably, much religious and moral education, with ever so noble goals, falls far short of this purpose. Why do we stuff heads with ethical content, while real Truth never seems to get to the heart and walk out into the streets as flesh and blood?

Those who have natural philosophies by and large appreciate the Hebrew model of Jesus, that the love of God and one's neighbor requires a definite content – the Law of God. But how is that love expressed except in life? The dialogue of love, which every Hebrew child knows (Deuteronomy 6), goes on informally from the doorway of the home to the gateway of the city. School has no hour, for it is in all of life, at places both sacred and profane, at the dinner or conference table, in a planned peripatetic experience in the city, or a walk, arm in arm, on a lovely river trail. It may include the exacting dialectic, adducing knowledge, or a maieutic experience, giving birth to self-knowledge. It is the early Greek model of Socrates rather than the scholastic model of the later Plato of the Academy or his student, Aristotle. The latter returned at the age of forty-four from the court of Philip the Great, to form his own school. It had the Aristotelian regimen, but also the discursive life of peripatetic philosophy.

The question: *Can this model be transferred into modern educational systems, given the human elements of inertia and institutional bureaucracy with its economic insecurity?* The most *compendious* description of Hebrew education is found in Ezra 7:10, where Ezra studied the law of God, practiced it, and then taught it. Ezra was first student himself, then an example, and then the creator of the schools, which eventually became synagogues. These were architecturally human-shaped, with a place for the teacher to sit down as Jesus did in the synagogue, on a boat, or on the mount. On the basis of a manageable portion of Scripture and commentary by a reader, the semi-circular *schule* lent itself to *dialogomai*. Dr. Luke describes this as Jesus opened His ministry in His hometown church at what was perhaps his *bar mitzvah*. Luke also uses the word *dialogomai* in recording Paul's "open discussion method" in his teaching ministry in the synagogues throughout the Roman Empire.

The most *comprehensive* description in a brief writing of how to teach the truth in a living way is found in the resurrection chapter of Luke's Gospel. One need not believe the claims of this passage to appreciate the remarkable teaching style described. The Master Teacher used a mentoring (discipleship) and small-group approach. After the stupendous events of the day, as the narrative describes – a resurrection after three days in a grave – one would expect a Cecil B. DeMille spectacular as the means to affect the world from that moment of triumph over man's mortal enemy. However, in what might be the greatest argument for a simple familial model for education, Jesus met with two unknown folks who were walking seven miles, and then later with a group of eleven people. He simply joined the sad travelers on a dusty road and asked questions. He was an intense listener, and He was ironic, letting His traveling friends persuade Him to stay and eat with them. It was a social and a spiritual event as He modeled the simple act of blessing a common meal. The teaching was in the village and the city, on the road, in a tavern, and a large home. Later, He taught them on a mountain, and the story ends with joy in the temple. The teaching style had unity in diversity, and the subsequent 2000 years of religious education shows its effectiveness.

Jesus taught that the Scriptures were true and dependable for life itself, and based on historic documents. He also taught from the Old Testament claims regarding both His Person and the Work of Redemption through death and resurrection. Though informal, there were dogmatics. He had two *table talks* that were intimate and informative, as well as inspirational – "Did not our hearts burn within us?" There was demonstration, encouragement, exhortation, honest rebuke, instruction, and promise – and He gave them a challenging vision to change the world through the Truth. They now had a plan, something to live for and something to die for. In all, it was the highest level of androgogy.

The crucial point I want to make is this. *The very nature of modern education precludes the dialogue and the Socratic enterprise, while human-shaped education with its manageable numbers includes them.* History is full of instructive examples, which encourage this kind of learning process. Like wisdom crying in the streets, they demand our earnest attention as Western Man and the whole World of Men hang in the balance. One such example is Oxford in the twelfth century, with its six colleges. We moderns would not be so impressed with the actual number of students – just 76. Each college was about twelve colleagues – the number that Jesus preferred. The Yale of Jonathan Edwards, one of the greatest intellects in American history, was a large colonial residence with a tutor (a generalist) and a handful of students. They worked and played, studied and prayed together as a community – the very elements of the undergraduate life so eloquently elevated in *The Idea of a Christian College* by Elton Trueblood.

One of the most notable examples of the holistic education of intimacy is that of Auguste Francke (b.1663) at the University of Halle in Germany. He had the religious devotion of his master, Philip Jacob Spener, and the scholarship of a Melancthon. He learned from Spener about the *collegium philobiblicum* – a college for Bible lovers. At Halle University his crowds grew to 300 students and professors. For personal depth, he brought some students into his home where they studied the Bible devotionally in Hebrew and Greek.

What were the results? Francke's life was that of a real man in real life in a university city, who maintained an *ethos* of compassion. He stretched his magnanimous heart in providing for homeless children, and discipled his students in God's love by this means. Francke's students ran a printing press to evangelize and a brewery (heavens!) to support it. They tutored the rich children for pay, in order to teach the poor children for free. They had an impact on the social institutions of the culture, and on the church as well. His orphanage was visited over a hundred years later by the most famous of all in the history of childcare. This work of faith and love became the model for George Mueller of Bristol, who at one point provided for over two thousand waifs. Another Englishman, in the line of Providence, benefited as well, and the overflow gave moral direction and courage to the American Colonies. Count Nicolas Von Zinzendorf, the leader of the Moravians, was a young student living in Francke's home. History is *writ large* as we see how one of his missionaries met John Wesley at Aldersgate with Luther's *Romans* in his hand, and the Methodist religious and social revolution began.

The dynamic *class meeting* of Wesley was nothing new, for the Moravians had modeled their groups after the early church. Incidentally, the primitive church had no buildings for its first two hundred years. The movements on the Continent and in England included the human-shaped church as well as human-shaped education. The pietists, reacting to the frigid scholasticism that followed Melancthon and Calvin, created the *ecclesia in ecclesiae,* the church in the church. Even as lectureship education reproduces lecture learning in the church and university, so this Hebrew model of Halle University produced pockets of moral power in the small group and in the covenant homes of the people. Such a *collegium* is a cogent call for a drastic reform in education in the *modern-postmodern* and beyond, especially that education which is termed "religious."

In the preparation of men and women for an adequate worldview made incarnate with wise and courageous action in the world, what is more necessary than this – that the mentor fill their minds with the Truth, flesh it out in his or her daily life, and thus earn the right to speak that Truth with moral persuasion? The disciples in turn had a word for their contemporaries, which had the ring of truth. The lifestyle of the moral and ethical teacher is the platform from which he or she speaks to his or her own generation with prophetic power. Those are the teachers who are in an ongoing conversation with the world of men, who know the issues of an orderly universe, which eventually ratify that which is the *True*, the *Good*, and the *Beautiful*.

What the World Needs Today Is a *Neo-Monastic Movement*

In the age of Thomas Aquinas, in the second millennium after Christ, there were monasteries holding divine and classical treasures, but a great divorce had taken place. They were either ingrown and scholastic, or aggressively mission and service-minded. The Cluny monasteries (the St.

Bernard-type) were termed *stabilitas*, being inward and scholastic – and that was good in itself. The Franciscans were termed *mobilitas*, being outward and mission oriented, and that was good in itself. But the best and safest way is the combination of the two. The scholastics were not too much on dialogue or community, indulging eternally in unwarranted speculation, lacking erudition and the principles of investigation. Aquinas knew neither Greek nor Hebrew, and appealed to tradition and rationalism. Augustine's Plato was lost to Aristotle's metaphysics and dialectics in Thomistic thought. As Francis Schaeffer says in *Escape From Reason,* nature had eaten up grace; reason presided over revelation. When the rational, empirical, and scientific come to their end, then man makes the fatal jump into the boneless arms of *irrationalism.*

But those who know the truth stand firm and take action – this is what keeps a movement pure, and that is not possible without community, the primary kind.

Rather than looking at the later monasticism, the Irish among us would be elated that we begin in the sixth century with Saint Patrick. Yet such ethnic green euphoria is blunted considerably by the fact that Patrick was English, living as a child near the Thames in England, and that in his day, the people of Ireland were called Scots. As a youngster Patrick was carried away to Ireland as a slave-boy. He cared for swine like the prodigal, and coming to the end of himself, he learned to pray as he cried to the Unknown God for help. The answer to his prayer made him a believer. Somehow he got a job caring for dogs being carried to France on an ill-fated commercial enterprise. The merchants, while in Normandy, were unable to obtain food even for themselves, much less the dogs. They asked Patrick to call on his God. He did, and some wild boars came along just in time. He felt that this contribution paid for his shipping, so he eventually ended up in the house of the kind Bishop Germanus in France, Gaulish churchman, bishop of Auxerre (*circa* 418 A.D.). St. Patrick was under his tutelage for fourteen years. His education was in the episcopal *familia,* which was the way of theological education until the middle of the nineteenth century when seminaries were invented. Protestant ministerial students "read theology" living with the pastor as Samuel Hopkins did with Sara and Jonathan Edwards.

When Patrick felt a call to take the Gospel to the children of Ireland, whose sad condition then was similar to his as a lad, Germanus refused him until a later time. Patrick was still *rusticas* (rustic, not yet genteel). Yet in time he had become an erudite and great-hearted bishop, commissioned by Germanus to return to Ireland to establish works of mercy and eventually agrarian monasteries. He instituted classical studies and thus Latin was preserved in its purity. Being distinct from Gaelic, Latin was not mongrelized as in Italy, France and Spain where it was being assimilated into the romantic languages. Being similar, continental dialects had blurred the distinctions of Latin's precise and punctilious grammar. The Irish monasteries, more like manors, were pastoral and missionary centers where learning in the arts, education, the Bible and humanities were cherished and communicated within the culture and transplanted in new centers. And there was marriage and families.

From Ireland Columbanus went to France and set up (the reader please note) **monastic houses** – rarely over twelve persons – which in turn became mission centers. These flourished in Burgundy, Italy, and what is now Switzerland where a recent study center movement began. Small monastic houses were easy to plant and multiply because they required only a large residence and a few students gathered around one mentor. In a *neo-monastic* movement for modernity, the same would hold true.

Incidentally, it is interesting to note that in the last part of the last century, the L'Abri study center movement was founded by Francis Schaeffer, who, like Patrick (sent from France to Ireland as a children's missionary), went to France from America to minister to children.

The most compelling story of the monastic centers is that of Columba, who went as a missionary to the Picts (Gaelic Scots of today). But he was an educational missionary, combining learning with mission. On the island of Iona a "study center" was founded. It was small by intention, because it kept sending out its educational evangelists. Aidan went into Northumbria in England, and from that humble beginning came the Venerable Bede, a godly classicist and historian who translated the Bible into the dialect, wrote a history of the English people, and was the intellectual and spiritual grandfather of Alcuin, the mentor of Charlemagne.

Charlemagne inherited a great legacy, being the grandson of Charles Martel, the courageous victor over the Moors in the Battle of Tours. As he consolidated the family empire, he wanted not only to conquer bodies and kingdoms, but hearts and minds, monasteries and churches. He sent for Alcuin in Northumbria, perhaps the most learned man in Europe, and from that point a small *renaissance and reformation* ensued conjointly. Thus the holistic monastic movement of service to people and education for the mind begun by Patrick, returned to France via England after some 200 years. It was mature and tested. Charlemagne called for the classics to be taught in his palace by Alcuin, and commanded that the Bible be read and followed. The historian Walker says that the passionate and scholarly Alcuin recruited "a company of likeminded scholars – a school of liberal arts in the palace."

With Alcuin, *Charles the Great* began to reorganize the monasteries for both learning and the practice of virtue, according to the God of the Scriptures. Each archbishop was to reform the church by turning his *familia* into a school. We are reminded here that the Dean (Fr. *deien,* "head of ten") of the Cathedral led a Chapter of Ten who were engaged by covenant in the learning discipline. Again, this is a human-shaped, manageable educational group. It then expanded into the monastic school, with growing libraries which preserved and passed on both the classical and the patristic literature, as well as Greek and Latin.

There was a Presbyter in various greater parishes who established the learning institutions not just for the clergy, *but for literacy among the general population.* The collegiate churches (inter-related through education and the Presbyter) gave the *unity* and *diversity* for the creation of *a university.*

The evidence of history is overwhelming. The great educational foundations which we now enjoy are standing on the shoulders of small learning centers known as monasteries, Cathedral Schools, or the *familias* in the houses of the educated bishops.

***May we infer that the cherishing of the modern study center
movement, which, though small, which if nurtured could provide
one of the keys to the survival of modern society as we know it?***

The Carolingian revival was both *renaissance* and *reformation,* and Charlemagne, with the evangelical and scholarly monasteries, almost preempted Florence and Geneva. Yet today, the resources of a medium-sized denomination, a university or a small state are far beyond those of that awesome figure. The ways and means of educational reform are not available as some sort of "instant replay." They are at hand for those who join an historical perspective with a present creativity, courage, and perseverance.

The Shape of the Study Center

There is a second part to this essay not included here, *a symposium* which transpires in Geneva, with Socrates, Jesus, Kierkegaard, and Carl Rogers agreeing that the *criteria* of *Truth, Beauty,* and *Goodness* was sufficient for making judgments regarding education. There is an orderly universe composed of these elements, and they serve well the corresponding ability of man to know what is true, good, and beautiful. Let us think of these ideas in relation to the study center. The following points are from the "notes" which Soren Kierkegaard took in the dreamlike "Symposium" in Part II.

- Man has a **body** and therefore education should have regard to bodily needs – rest, exercise, eating. And there should be more than merely sustaining the body. Elton Trueblood suggests that the college cafeteria, so very convenient with its fast food, is perhaps a curse. Dining and lively conversation is virtually unknown as the nurturer of social and intellectual development. A room, chairs, their arrangement, comfort and all of that which is appropriate must be in the planning for good education because man is a physical being. Princeton University created the dining environments where the comestible experience would engender sociability and mutual disquisition.

Comment: A study center in a home, a chalet, or manor house creates a physical environment suitable to man's physical being. One must sit near others. One finds himself with others around a table for common meals where table talk and mutual learning may transpire. Such intimacy is a necessity for social progress and a positioning for moral learning and dialogical thinking.

- Man has a **will** that needs training, which eventuates in the self-governing virtue of Socratic *sophosphrune* or temperance.

Comment: The familial environment calls for accountability along with warmth and intimacy. It has been my experience that some are forced to flee community from fear of the personal, while others are forced to change through the power of the personal. Large commercial educational institutions that merchandise in transcripts and body counts can claim no moral commitment created out of meaningful relationships. *The will, unchecked through social accountability and mutual love, even in the best of us, is on an entropic roller coaster.*

- Man has a physical **brain** that records *data* and a **mind** that thinks. Man needs food for the brain (content), and contradictions and antitheses for the mind to create thought.

Comment: As Carl Mannheim said, "Thinking is not a solitary matter." In large lecture halls, people are alone. But in a study center, the dialogue naturally ensues, and from this happening, thoughts are born. E. I. Rhone points out that because of this, a small movement like the L'Abri Fellowship (scarcely 200 *active* participants) has produced more Christian books that are culturally significant than fifty Christian liberal arts colleges conjointly. In this statement he did not mean there are not many excellent offerings from the religious institutions such as technical research and textbooks. Perhaps he did not know that Calvin College has spoken to the culture through many studies and books produced by its *think tank*.

In terms of the intimate, face-to-face situation created in the study center where people may play and pray, work and think together, and be in constant dialogue over ideas, we must agree that Socrates and Jesus have been excellent examples. Their *maieutic* midwifery assisted the birth of thought through riddles and questions, parables and irony, both in words and deeds. Perhaps we modern educators should rapidly advance to the past, if we dare.

- Man is a **moral being,** and his oft-perverted will demands a moral and ethical education. Plato regarded it a danger to the Republic if an educated man lacked justice.

Comment: In a community of scholars, the moral and ethical dimensions are forever challenged and stretched. Here deeds are better than words, and *being* is better than *doing*. One is scarcely discipled from afar or by the Homeric heroes of the past or by store window saints. One must learn morality in the small (primary) group or perish from an obdurate heart.

- Man is a **social being** and therefore there should be a social *milieu*, an environment of mutual caring for one another's minds and persons – a reciprocity of learning. We remind you that Margaret Meade concluded that true learning was not with vertical, piped down transmission, but through lateral transmission, shared learning with mutual caring for the other's growth.

Comment: This is already alluded to, but if the family is the place for social training, the study center obviously provides a setting for further development of social interest, mutual caring, collegiality, and loving the mind of one's neighbor as his own. For some, it is a second chance, and a golden opportunity for re-training for living graciously. The High Tea on Sunday afternoon at L'Abri was Edith Schaeffer's grand *schemata* for teaching more than mere words.

Plato believed that the highest education required not only instruction and training, but also *fellowship* . . . a way of life as a condition for achieving conversion – a change of mind. For the Socratic dialectic, at least two persons are needed in a social relationship known as the *pedagogical eros* of mutual love – a machine and a person won't do. Plato shows that it takes dialogue to integrate domestic, economic and political roles in a virtuous and just person.

- Man is an **aesthetic being**, and must cultivate taste for the arts and culture, or his education is far short of his destined greatness.

Comment: In a small group, one can discuss beauty, and also ugliness. In the very mobility of it, "Let's take a holiday at the museum or in the mountains," the added content of beauty and reality is appreciably increased. One's ability to experience different forms of beauty, and thus aesthetic feelings and perceptions, may be all the more enhanced. I took a study center group with Dr. Grady Spires of Gordon College (the consummate peripatetic lecturer) to the Goya Exhibit at the Fine Arts Museum in Miami. One young artist, by his own appraisal, has since entered into an era of tremendous creativity because of that personal, small-group time with a living voice in the matrix of the museum. The group had its discussion over *cafe con leche* in a Cuban restaurant – indeed one of the pleasures of a true education in a Latin culture.

- Man is a **spiritual being,** and therefore the depths of his soul must be plumbed regarding God, being, non-being, mortality, immortality, destiny – the metaphysical "things unseen" which all of this implies. Even the atheist who is secure enough to risk the dialogue will learn much in open, mutual disquisitions in religious thought.

Comment: A study center, since man apparently is a spiritual being and is almost universally religious, *must* not deny what Whitehead cites as *a call of the university* – to engender loyalty and reverence in the student.

A **Christian** study center must do more than conform it into humanity—it must conform to divinity. It must introduce revelation in Jesus Christ, the Word of God, and on that content build a theological worldview grid with which to see and think Christianly. It calls for a lifestyle of walking in the truth and courageously applying the truth to the critical issues of society.

- Man is also ***hominem ludens,*** **Man, the Player**. Therefore, learning should not be labor alone, but there is a time for sheer enjoyment with the spontaneity of a kitten.

Comment: There is no doubt that creativity and **re**-creation are connected. Brewster Ghiselin in *The Creative Process* presents varied and remarkable analyses of the self-conscious statements of Mozart, Einstein, Poncare' and other such geniuses, and arrives at this principle: After intense times of concentration, during subsequent moments of leisure, the insight, the *eureka,* breaks from the unconscious into the conscious. Interestingly enough, the word for school comes from the Greek *skole,* which means leisure, and the implications are obvious. I would only add the words of one of my students at the International School of Theology who was in the Core Module (a human-shaped learning group): "Those other guys in the regular class are jealous . . . they don't think we should be having so much fun."

- Man is also a ***political being***, derived from his social, moral, and willful nature. Therefore this very nature demands some sort of order for his proper function, and for survival itself – the necessity for civilization. Moreau states and proves that the Greek purpose in education was to produce good citizens. A Christian community should go far beyond that, especially as we have lost the *civil* in civilian. The last time I held a chair for a lady she almost fainted.

Another time I held the car door feeling quite gallant, and the good the lady was irate for impugning her equality.

Comment: In human-shaped education and study centers, we have discovered that the idea of government, the chain of command, headship, eldership, and the rule of law are being learned by the very nature of the small *collegium*. A formal curriculum on the science of politics is not necessarily needed. Socrates said that the major aspect of Greek education was political, in that no man could escape the *polis*. Greek education (as Carl Rogers said of John Dewey's educational philosophy) was principally intended to make good citizens. The moral and social aspect of man demands that he not be an *apolitical* animal. These social beings are not perfect, so they need legislation and accountability, which demand some political structure. Rousseau and the anarchists would not agree with the majority that even an inferior form of government is better than none.

The only statement more ignorant than "I don't talk about politics" is "I don't talk about religion." The freedom to talk or not to talk today in America and Russia exists because the Jeffersons and the Yeltsins did talk about it. To speak about religion gives insight for freedom of the man in the Kingdom of the Heart; to speak about politics nurtures freedom for the kingdoms of this world.

For Reflection

I could make no higher recommendations for the reader of this historical essay than to read Newman's *Idea of the University,* Whitehead's *The Aim of Education,* and Elton Trueblood, who educated until ninety-three years of age, "The Idea of a College" and "The Redemption of the College" (**A Philosopher's Way**; Broadman, 1978). Here Trueblood, reflecting a Quaker heritage and his experience in the small college, has eloquently and cogently set forth all the aspects of the Christian Study Center which we have discovered as valid in our on-site visits, as reported in the Appendix of these papers. He demonstrates that the *college* must be true to Man as he is, or it cannot be true to its educational calling. The **Christian college** must also be true to God, or it will fail in its redemptive calling **"as a conscious effort to avoid the decay of civilization and to make that civilization worthy of permanence."**

There are necessary differences between a study center and a larger institution, and each has its proper place.

- The study center is versatile, and may exist in the village, the country, on a mountaintop or the city.
- The study center is free from academic accreditation, and therefore is able to develop the curriculum that suits its mission and those whom it serves.
- The study center is so human (not socially engineered or pedagogically programmed) that it offers an open forum for discussion, for both the seeking doubter and the doubting believer.
- A study center is dynamic – forever growing and multiplying children in its image, as the monasteries of the sixth through the eighth centuries show, or those modern types such as L'Abri or the Torchbearer Centers.
- A study center is economical, and demands neither large budgets nor grand tuitions. It needs no government grants, but a handful of loyal sacrificial folks at the heart of it in who share both faith and love. If one falls, the others may assist it. If it falls ultimately, it takes none with it, for it is but a small thing. Great churches, universities, colleges and conference centers are forever on the auction block or in crisis. Churches like mausoleums and educational centers without the grants become Grants Tombs. We weep with David, "How have the mighty fallen?", for each has had a significant contribution before its demise.
- A Christian study center is covenantal, and is sustained by the grace of forgiveness, mutual love and respect, service, and cherishes the Gospel call through hospitality. It is a living thing. It is a blessed extended family.

A Shining Conviction

The Christian Church should begin to combine evangelism and education, ministry and the Christian mind, in launching a study center movement in strategic nations and cities worldwide, focusing wherever possible on the national capitals and the great universities. In the later case it is the *Cluster College* reborn as in the founding of Oxford, Cambridge, and the *Sorbonne*. Such Christian Study Centers can renew the Great Conversation called for by Chancellor Hutchins, with two grand confidences:

- *First, Christianity is not a religion; it is the **Truth of the Universe**. The blunt logic is this: History, science, art and literature, when dialectically examined, given time and events, will yield homage to that **Truth**.*
- *Secondly, Jesus Christ is God with skin on – He entered history, lived and died for men as they are, and **the third day He rose from the dead**. Mere mortals can know the Living God!*

The study center that is genuinely Christian may go far beyond the *Great Conversation.* It will be mighty on the earth in terms of fulfilling the *Great Commission,* and a supreme joy in heaven to the God who sent His Son to redeem it. In the light of that sacrifice, would you who read run with the vision, to take up the challenge of the first generation Christians to *"out-think, out-live, and out-die"* our own post-Christian generation?

Chapter 14

THE STUDY CENTER AS A COVENANT COMMUNITY

This is an oral essay presented to the founding body of the Bronx Household of Faith Study Center, a Covenant Community dedicated to communicating and implementing God's perspective in the postmodern-postChristian world, through critical theological inquiry and dialogue in the marketplace of men and ideas, and by living out the Christian life together in a ministry of loving service and faithful proclamation of the Gospel in everyday life.

Celebrating a House Church and an Urban Study Center

This is a remarkable occasion as we consider what kind Providence has brought us together this night, so full of hope and excited at growing our minds and hearts in the love of God through a Christian Study Center in the Bronx – easier might a tree grow in Brooklyn. Yet in hearing the story of each one of you, God has planted you in the city, and you have found your *shalom* as you have sought the welfare of this great city within a city.

Al Santino as a young Christian at Rutgers heard me on the radio 15 years earlier on "Winds from the Northeast" (Star 99.1) and opted for the city as his service. Then I was called to the School of Theology in California and he was there as a student librarian. We agreed to walk the streets together to share the Good News and study the city. Moving to the Bronx and seeking how to minister, I recommended he meet the team of Hall and the Roberts, now pastoring the Bronx Household of Faith. We met these committed pastors in 1973 on the Ocean Grove Beach where we were just having fun with our Columbia Bible College students. Now God has brought us together. May the Lord bless your hearts and minds as we seek to think His thoughts after Him.

The Study Center as a Covenant Community

The Covenant provides the most complete context for a Christian community. From it comes righteousness (a right standing with God), regeneration (a new heart for God) and redemption (daily forgiveness and grace from God and for each other). These three provide for man as a Redeemed social being to live with others with common purpose in the practice of the Truth.

What is the Covenant? O. Palmer Robertson states it succinctly. "It is a bond in blood sovereignly administered. It is a Triune Covenant of the Triune God, first in the counsels of eternity and then in space in time with His Covenant people. The Father's Sovereign Plan is centered in the Redeeming Blood-Covenant of Christ through His Own Blood, and that administered among men by the Holy Spirit of God."

The Covenant provides us the "The Three R's" for the community known as the Church –

RIGHTEOUSNESS is above us. The Covenant assures us that Christ is our Righteousness, that He is before the Father, the same yesterday, today and forever. Whatever one's state as a redeemed man or woman, whether the condition is up or down, one thing never changes: Christ, our Righteousness, *Jehovah-Tsidkenu*. How wonderful that in our daily lives full of broken promises and broken laws, we can look to heaven and see Jesus, resplendent before the Father, our holiness, and our acceptance. In our most laggardly and dissolute times as Christians, we are and always will be justified by faith. It is better than Adam's innocence, sinless but untried. It is a righteousness tested in every point as we are, yet without sin. It is God's righteousness, and God cannot reject God or a Perfect Man, risen from the dead. This keeps community intact because it is in Christ.

REGENERATION is the gift of a new life because of Christ's righteousness, a necessary Covenant promise. Christ comes with RIGHTEOUSNESS in one hand and REGENERATION in the other. God willingly gives us His Holy Spirit who takes all the things of Christ – His love, His joy, His peace, His patience, and He makes them ours in all of life—a worldview. Here is the power and grace to live out the Christian life, i.e., the Risen Lord living out His Life, in terms of our redeemed personalities. This creates a colony of heaven on earth in the family and community, and in turn, sends such light and truth into the marketplace. It should be the experience of the believer and unbeliever alike as they enter the community of God's people that "surely the Presence of the Lord is in this place."

REDEMPTION is the bedrock of blood, sweat and tears living. We are fallen saints lifted up, living in a fallen world. A family or study center cannot survive idealism: that sweet idol of Pollyanna Christianity that says the family, the church or community ought to be this way or that. Where we live is where we sin and make countless little errors, great mistakes, and even gross ones. As an agnostic poet friend says rightly, "We are damaged goods." And I add, we damage lots of other goods, especially those called children: and they seem to pass it on.

Bonhoeffer writes in *Life Together*, that the ideal becomes an idol, and we determine to follow that idol to its logical conclusion: first when it doesn't work out in the real world, we get critical and angry with others, then with God, and finally with ourselves. How may we avoid this spiritual adultery and idolatry and save untold human misery?

With Christ's Righteousness <u>above</u> us, His Regeneration <u>within</u> us, and His Redemption <u>beneath</u> us, we live with pardon, power and purity. What Redemption meant in our family was not having to be perfect: Christ is all of that. We did not have to live in our own strength; Christ imparted that by His Holy Spirit. But where we sin and fail, there is Redemption, unshakable and mighty. I have been forgiven forever and may be forgiven today. I can come and confess my sins to God and discover that the Blood of Jesus keeps on cleansing me from all sin. I can go to my wife, colleagues or friends finding and giving forgiveness, and it is all because of the Cross. As Bonhoeffer also said, "We can accept and forgive one another not for what we are, but in the hope of all that we yet shall be." With Redemption can we find room as imperfect people to get up and live again. We are beyond failure and never beyond Christ.

**The Covenant gives the community a perfect Righteousness,
a New Life, and Redemption, and it must be
Triune Truth – *it cost God His Son.***

Unity and Diversity

The beauty of L'Abri came to be as Francis and Edith Schaeffer innocently received friends of their college children weekend after weekend with all their questions. This diversity of seeking people was a tapestry, and yet, it was all of one piece – the Truth held it together. Out of this grew the philosophy which had real answers for the real world we live in. There the Schaeffers realized existentially that Christianity was not a religion at all, but the Truth of the Universe.

The Christian Study Center has no wrong people and no wrong questions. Seeking to know God, standing firm in the Truth and taking action with the Truth, the old and young, intellectual and undereducated, seekers of all classes, gender, race and groups are welcomed as they are, all in the hope of what they yet shall be. "The Truth shall set you free." There is no one who is not to be cherished. Yet without accountability and discipline being added to that intimacy of communal life, any community or family is doomed to failure. Community Life is the given, but what are the tools of the study center enterprise in order to communicate and implement the God's perspective on Man's world?

The Tools of Learning

Dorothy Sayers wrote a remarkable essay of the above title, and we would honor her in some of the necessities for any person or community seeking to know Truth. These tools must be utilized in a context of worship. Without hearts given to the glory of God, tools are mere methods, creating craven and empty creatures locked into facts and figures, a blind sort of formula faith, but not having the substance of Truth. These seekers serve one another, sharing love with each other and with the world at large. Francis Bacon said, and we paraphrase: Reading and listening (tape libraries were not in Bacon's day) make a full man; conversation a ready man; and writing an exact man.

A study center needs books and the time and place for reading them; all else will fail without this. Lectures are also significant for the input needed. There must be dialogue: informal and formal. In classrooms, table talk, high tea, on the mountain, in the forest, at the beach, restaurants and taverns, and living rooms by the fire: in places sacred and profane. This develops critical thinking, facile minds, and always better, faster, more retentive readers, well documented by research. But it is the writing that makes the exact man. No fuzzy thought can escape the inexorable "there-ness" of the printed page. The essay (Fr. coinage of Montaigne, "an attempt") is one of the great tools of learning; neither pedantic nor romantic, it allows for passion and truth, and for expression without a stuffy "bookishness". It sticks to the subject and allows a bit of digression. The study center will fail without it. And how wonderful to have essays read around the dinner table: the best of desserts.

With the threefold cord of the head for Truth, the heart for Love, and the Hand for obedience, literally "doing theology," the community of the Holy Spirit cannot be broken. The love and action of heart and hand will confirm the acquisitions of the Head. Critical thought requires the best of Descartes' methodical doubt and that of Socrates in his maieutic (midwife) approach to seeking for the Absolute. We have noted elsewhere that *Maieutikos* is the Greek word used by Socrates whose mother was a midwife. That is what it means, and that is precisely what he did: not create thought-babies, but assist them to be born.

Communicating God's Perspective: Jerusalem And Athens

Aristotle gave us three words in his rhetoric, which I elevate in all writings on education. One readily sees their relevance to all of communication, a universal at any time and place and culture: *Ethos, Pathos, and Logos.*

To communicate without *ethos* is like a body with no bones. There is no true hidden strength to what is said. There must be character to sustain the telling of truth. Without that, it is turned into lying and hypocrisy. The communicator with integrity (Gr. *integere*, lit. untouched, therefore without blemish and whole as an integer, a whole number) brings an open ambiance, an atmosphere of trust to the marketplace of Truth and Ideas. This person at all times and seasons is the same in the core of his or her being. A message about Truth would not be taken seriously when told by a liar, or one on purity when told by the licentious one. A Greek proverb says, "the greatest of the Good is to Be." Not bad remembering that the verb "to be" is the very name of God, the True and Faithful God.

However, to tell the Truth without *pathos* or passion is like placing a roller coaster on a flat surface: it gets nowhere. Yet another proverb says that "No heart is so pure that it is not passionate; no virtue safe that is not enthusiastic" (Lit. "God breathed"). If someone of good character came into this room and in a lackadaisical, lethargic, apathetic manner said in Alabama slowness, "The house is on fire," one may not be moved to move. Even a liar with great passion could trick everyone to rush out mindlessly: such is the way of the demagogue. The great teacher has passion for the Truth, which is the Subject. But the best of all he also has passion for the object, the which is the student. Jesus beheld both the young ruler and the multitudes and was "moved with compassion." So often actors speak with conviction so that the unreal becomes real. Often Christians speak as actors, making the real unreal. We need lovers of God and neighbor, heart, mind, soul, and strength at street level, the "naked public square" and in the university, as well as at the dinner table.

From whence the *ethos* of character? It flourishes in an atmosphere of intimacy and accountability, as at a covenant community of a study center, or in the daily life of a covenant Christian family. The Greeks derived from Homer merely two qualities, loyalty and courage, but their gods gave them impure and inconsistent character, for, as Augustine said, "Their gods are made in their image." Mutual respect, acceptance, service to each other, grace and forgiveness, with the courage of holding others responsible for words and deeds – this can do it!

At the universities, as we speak of this. I tell the secular and sincere brothers that this may be a spiritual issue, a theological enterprise. God alone can supply the needed *ethos*. And where is the requisite love, the caring, the *pathos* that gives power to Truth and to Character? We embrace the love that produces love, then dwell together on God who is love and practice the Truth in Love: The Apostle Paul sent forth by the Antioch community and always serving in community left bloody footprints on all the seashores of the Empire, "He loved ME, and gave Himself for ME was his cry." A Covenant family or community is the womb of those lovely twins of integrity and love.

Logos ("wisdom") is a necessity. Although God can do without our intelligence, He can do less with our ignorance. Bob Dylan said that he wants to know his tune before he tries to sing it. There must be fact, information, and truth. There must be skill at gathering information, systematizing it, and after researching and writing to do more of the same, an endless calling. Teachers of the *logos* make a school famous. They work hard, go to conferences, get advanced degrees, read books, but they must think about this world of order and purpose, and think on the world to come. The *Logos* of the Bible is Christ, "lighting every man that comes into the world: in whom are hid all the treasures of wisdom and knowledge."

Again, it seems that the "thesaurus," the pond, the reservoir for Truth, is best contained in the TRUTH. Again a theological calling is in character and love. A friend of Eldridge Cleaver came for ten days to our Study Center. He said he was an atheist, but it was not so. He was a soft-core agnostic who loved reading *Basic Christianity* by John Stott and listening to Francis Schaeffer, reading the Bible every morning and listening to others pray. This man says that nowhere in the world could he have learned of love and life, and sought for truth as in a place like our frail, all-too-human community.

To know one's song without *ethos* and *pathos* is to sing with a cacophonous tune with no rest notes. But these two without the *logos* is to have no song at all. The Neo-Gnostics of the New Age have some love, and occasional character, but no one else can sing their song, because it has no substance, and it has no harmony: only individual experience which cannot be communicated. No "New-Ager" or Hindu can remain the same in a Covenantal Study Center because of the power of the Covenant made with the Mighty Son of God before the world began, and lived out on the bedrock of Redemption by His people.

Let me comment that combining the best of the dialogue method, the Socratic enterprise, Jesus, Kierkegaard, Carl Rogers, Dostoyevsky, and Columbo (not their worldviews) is the best way to develop thought, retain it, and stand on Truth in the marketplace. The maieutic way creates thinkers instead of automatic "fact vending machines" who rob your quarters in the marketplace. Thesis and antithesis, with the presupposition that there is ABSOLUTE TRUTH leaves the thesis unchanged, while the antithesis is drawn inexorably toward the truth, as false ideas are discarded. The way of the midwife is fun, with irony, humor, and good nature. It is serious; it is a life-and-death matter. It is of all the ways of learning "the most humane." (Cudsworth, 1654). Without Truth, all approaches that are relative are endless digressions into the unknown, finally creating mindless mice on a treadmill.

The *logos* comes by diligence, earnestness, ardor, blood, sweat and tears. All the character and passion in the world without it would be like a passionate lover offering the beloved nothing in a golden goblet. Character and love are no substitute for that which is true. They are all one threefold cord which must not and cannot be broken.

Why then should there be a study center in the Bronx near the formidable Fordham University, or next to the University of Mexico with its 400,000 students? But I ask you, why should there not be? That is the question.

If there must be **Truth, Beauty and Goodness** to educate, and *Ethos, Pathos and Logos* to communicate God's perspective—*the Christian world and life view*, let us seize the moment! Shakespeare gives the challenge well in the words of the pagan Mark Anthony to sly old Cassius.

"The enemy increaseth every day, and we are diminished. There is a tide in the affairs of men, which, taken at the flood, leads on to fortune; omitted, all the voyage of their journey is bounded by shallows and miseries. We are now on such a sea afloat, and we must take the current while it serves or lose the ventures before us."

All the more cogent are the words of the eminent world Christian, the multicultural and trilingual Jew, Greek and Roman – the Apostle Paul. These mighty words wrenched the *Confessions* out of Augustine and presented us with *The City of God*. May they become ours!

Now you must act, knowing the time – it is now high time to awake out of sleep; for now our salvation is nearer than when we first believed. The night is far spent; the day is at hand. Let us therefore cast off the works of darkness and put on the armor of light! Let us walk properly, as in the day, not in revelry or drunkenness, not in lewdness and lust, not in strife and envy, but put on the Lord Jesus Christ, making no provision for the flesh, to fulfill its lusts. (Romans 13:11-14).

Although he was ready, a debtor, and unashamed of the power of the Gospel, he might well be ashamed of the languid, "born again" Christians delivered at the church door brain dead!

A Personal Note

As for me, I feel at this point in life I have just begun, and at this point with whatever gifts and strength I have, I want to dedicate all I am and have to the Lord Jesus, extending the reign of Christ in heads and hearts through Christian Education and the Everlasting Gospel.

Ulysses said it well with son Telemachus in the presence of the old warrior after returning from the Trojan War:

> *Come, my friends, 'tis not too late to seek a newer world.*
> *Push off, and setting well in orders*
> *we shall smite the sounding furrows*
> *and sail beyond the baths of all the Western stars.*
> *It may be that the gulfs will wash us down;*
> *It may be, that we shall touch the Happy Isles*
> *And see the great Achilles whom we knew.*
> *And although we are not that strength,*
> *which of old moved earth and heaven,*
> *That which we are, we are,*
> *One equal spirit of heroic hearts,*
> *To seek, to strive, to find,*
> *And not to yield.*

If the pagans will say that with such bravado, then I will pray with David, "Now that I am old, let me show Thy strength to this generation . . ." And Moses would add, "These are not mere words, they are your life."

CHAPTER 15

EDUCATION AND THE CITY: A MODEST PROPOSAL

Proposal: *That the Core Module Education Model be adopted as an interdisciplinary theological study track for first year pastoral M.Div. students and qualified undergraduates with five years of ministry experience at both evangelical and pluralistic seminaries.*

Background: *The Urban Year program was born in 1973 at New York Theological Seminary and developed in New Jersey by Rev. William T. Iverson, Ph.D., the writer of this proposal. Bill Iverson is a graduate of Davidson College, Columbia Theological Seminary, with a Ph.D. in Religious Education from New York University; he has served as professor in sociology and theology, and Vice President of Ministry in a graduate seminary. Mainly he has lived and served in the city for forty-five years of ministry, and had a part in the start-up of over fifteen churches, including Spanish, Brazilian, and African-American. He has worked with "turnaround churches" and most recently with Trinity Reformed, Newark, growing from five congregants to seventy-five adherents and members. He has maintained first and foremost a covenant family as the center of Christian ministry with the Reformed perspective as the basis of his biblical worldview and his philosophy of ministry. He believes that theology is practical, and must be applied to ministry and everyday life or it is lifeless and useless. He also knows that apart from the Holy Spirit, there is no ministry, and that which does not point to the glory of Christ is unworthy of this high calling.*

The Core Module is a theological education model that lends itself to the fullest integration of theory and practice, the cognitive and affective, intimacy and accountability, yet meeting the demands of academia. Dr. Bill Webber, President of New York Theological Seminary, commissioned Bill Iverson to develop the Urban *Year,* a core group of twelve students learning in intimacy and accountability as a congregation-in-mission. The classical and practical disciplines were taught together, approximating a first-year graduate seminary program. It was in this same period of time that Dr. Webber advised the then-President of New Brunswick Theological Seminary, Dr. Howard Hagaman, to change the *schemata* of the seminary program and adapt to new target groups, as to age and ethnicity.

Dr. Donald Clarke, Academic Dean of the International School of Theology in Kenya, did his Ph. D. dissertation (University of Texas) on Core Module Education. After two years of intense clinical observation of the Core Modules developed by Bill Iverson at the International School of Theology, Dr. Clarke defended and demonstrated that this form of education puts together in one model most, if not all, of the attempts at reform in the history of theological education. His "Two-Thirds World" colleagues see this as indeed "human-shaped" and not an imposition of the Western, linear mind.

The Personnel for the Core Module are a Master-teacher and 10-15 students. Larger classes combine plenary lectures with the smaller segments, or make more use of the triad. In order to multiply the module, it is also good to have mentors, who are teachers-in-training. These may be pastors or theological professors with pastoral experience. This can be within a seminary program or a study center.

The Elements of Organization for Certificate Program Core Module

Let the educator note that the two-year certificate program described here is much like the original Urban Year program that Dr. Bill Webber developed, except it was a one-year intense program. This same program can be the first two semesters of a two-year M.A. or the three-year M.Div. degree to be accepted by a conventional seminary. A *Pastoral Theology* Track could be concurrent with the certificate program for undergraduates, only requiring more reading and writing and leading to the M.Div. or M.A. When the demands of accreditation are satisfied, the mature undergraduate practitioner enriches the program for the full-time graduate student. *Full-time graduate students can do this in one year.* The certificate Core Module is a four-semester, two-year program with twelve weeks per semester, ordinarily on Saturdays for four hours. Two courses are taught in an interdisciplinary manner.

The Core Module as declared a ***Congregation in Mission*** is one of New York Theological Seminary President Bill Webber's ingenious inventions for polity, evangelism, and mercy ministry for the "mini-church." The class elects (after due time) an Elder and a Deacon. This enables a focus on church polity, and with some reading and essays, may gain academic credit in that church administration, etc. The class becomes a worshiping assembly, ministering to the Lord, to one another, and to the world. There is both a stewardship of the Gospel and material means, so that it is a giving body of believers. The elder is in charge of worship, and the deacon of logistics and arrangements for retreats, meals, and meeting places, and of offerings for those in need. With the Master-teacher (and Mentors), these form a Consistory, which helps govern the congregation with discipline and direction, including ministerial and academic evaluation.

The Triads are small groups that meet not only during class, but 3-4 times per semester for reading essays in tutorials, with a mentor or the Master-teacher. The tutorial strengthens the Core Module process and gives depth of understanding. Intimacy and accountability with a godly thinker will develop critical Christian worldview thinkers who can write and speak well, discuss freely and honestly, while living, ministering and witnessing in a gracious and effective manner.

The environment for the class is ordinarily the seminary, and yet could meet in churches, beaches, mountains, libraries, government offices, businesses, courtrooms, hotels, restaurants, and homes or in a study center. The marketplace brings the student into the real world and also students are most at home at home. The students see one another in life, and especially learn life in the "open heart, open home" of the teacher and his family. Any time or any place is right for this kind of education. The classroom is where more time is concentrated, but the other venues in *modicum* make for a *continuum* of learning readiness.

The Methods of Core Module teaching conform to the "loving God" model of Deuteronomy 6 with the perspicuous example of Jesus. This is sound pedagogy found in the history of education from Socrates to Comenius to the present. In the many environments there may be lecture method, discussion, drama, visual aids (often the reality of poverty or a jail may be the visual aid), essays, research, group projects, surveys, table talks at meals, "doing" theology, ministry, and like Jesus, the nearest coin or little child will do. Transcultural and multi-class settings are often used to break students out of their comfort zones. The maieutic approach of Socrates and Jesus, the questioning and ironic midwifery of persons and ideas, is at the heart of the process.

Mortimer Adler and the *Paideia Proposal*

If there were any person in the past 100 years who would know the elements of true education, it would be Mortimer Adler, editor of both the *Encyclopedia Britannica* and *The Great Books of the Western World*. He also developed the St. John's Great Books curriculum and founded Paidea. Adler divides education into his famous "three columns" of the necessary elements of education. Most higher education limits itself to the first element and bits of the second and third. The first element is *didactic instruction and factual information,* which is mostly the lecture method; the second is *intellectual coaching of skills,* which is taught through coaching and supervised practice; the third element is *understanding ideas and values,* and this is acquired through the *maieutic* or midwife approach of Socrates with questioning and discussion, and it can be enhanced through drama, the arts, observation and discussion in peripatetic experiences. (See the Paideia Chart, Chapter 11) the core module includes in balance these three, and Kierkegaard, a Socratic writer, says that character development – the ethical, moral, and spiritual formation—must come through the maieutic way. This is approach is often employed by Jesus in religious dialogue and is at the heart of Carl Rogers' indirect counseling. There is a whole school of this pedagogy through the *Paideia Center* at the University of North Carolina. (Also see the dissertation, *The Maieutic Approach,* Iverson, 1976).

The Core Module Certificate Program

The Director: Qualifications- A Ph.D. and generalist with creditable pastoral experience, and a minister of the Word and Sacrament. To satisfy a particular denominational distinctive, he or she must be a minister in good standing in that communion.

Term: Two-year contracts

Duties:

- To organize the times and places of the approved classes, name teachers and mentors to be approved by the Dean or an appointed three-member committee; to receive and submit extensive syllabi of each course offered with the teacher's applications to personal development, spiritual formation, theology, churchmanship, and ministry;
- To teach at least one of the classes each semester, and to lead the integration table talks after each double session, usually at lunch on the Saturday at the seminary. *All classes should have a written handout teaching agenda, a useful tool for core module education of any academic class.*
- To organize triads, monitor triad meetings; create special learning events and environments, retreats, etc. In addition, exposing the students to relevant practitioners;

- To develop the *congregation in mission* with the elder-deacon components, and govern the class through this "consistory," the elder (s) taking spiritual leadership for devotionals and the class *ethos,* and the deacon (s) doing the logistical things— projectors, lunches, retreats, arrangements etc. *This may be developed as a church polity course with summer reading and writing assignments.*
- To develop stewardship plans to strengthen the funding for the program;
- To serve the Dean in *curriculum design* as needed;
- To submit written reports to the Dean or as required, and welcome a review of the program each semester, including student evaluations.

The Teaching Team: A Director, key seminary professors with pastoral experience, and adjunct academic pastors active in ministry form the teaching corps. Each class session will have a teacher and may have an assistant-in-training (volunteer, not salaried), a person who is rendering a service to the seminary for the full twelve-week semester. This will train mentors for the future of the program.

A mentor pool should be developed by gathering the biographical and academic data, recommendations, and evaluation of ministry effectiveness. Generally these will be non-salaried servants of the church.

The Curriculum

The courses are ordinarily taught in twelve four-hour sessions on Saturday mornings with other necessary stipulations of time being met through triads, mentoring sessions, retreats and projects.

Semester One
Old Testament and Church History

Semester Two
Life of Christ is coupled with *Discipleship/Servant Leadership*
(Note: By giving more time to the New Testament content, discipleship, evangelism, mission, and churchmanship gain a strong foundation.)

*SUMMERS: SPECIAL STUDY OPTIONS**

Semester Three
Acts and the Epistles with *Evangelism* and Ecclesiology

Semester Four
Systematic Theology with *Basic Hermeneutics* and *Biblical Exposition*
(Note: Example on Distinctives—Ongoing reading and studies on the confessions such as the Heidelberg Catechism and the Westminster Standards will be the doctrinal foundation for a Reformed and Presbyterian certificate.)

*Comment on the summer: A reading course on Ethics, Society, and Culture or a Demographic Project (with mentors) or Church Planting project could be a plus for the certificate program.

Notes on Credentialing

These courses should be of academic excellence so that with a grade given to an undergraduate or graduate, it could be used toward a degree. For instance, a student who is allowed to attend New York Divinity School (NYDS) in the graduate program without the undergraduate credentials could use these courses toward an M.A. or M.Div. certificate, and in the future, upon receiving a bachelor's degree, this could become the proper graduate degree. Columbia Theological Seminary has done this with great success. Undergraduate schools may also accept these courses by their own standards or through such processes as afforded by the Thomas Edison program. Of course, all of this is cost-effective by its very nature. Just one more thing, Francis Bacon had an educational maxim that is the heart of the program:

> **"Reading makes a full man; conversation a ready man; writing an exact man."**

APPENDIX

A Study Center Pilgrimage: An Experiential Assessment

The Providence of Our Journey

On May 1, 1988, the Bill Iverson family moved from Crestline, California to Miami, Florida, into a lovely *art deco* house in Little Havana. There was an unformed idea that this would be a place where interns, students, pastors and missionaries might visit for study and ministry in Miami in a transcultural setting, and where persons could find repose and encouragement. We have done this informally for forty years. We ministered as stated supply at our home church, Shenandoah Presbyterian, in seeking to help re-plant the church in its present Latin community. As we completed that *interim,* there was a distinct sense that we should go to Europe in the Spring of 1990 for broadening in our lives. Naturally, there was no focus and certainly no justifying economic or ministry purpose that could possibly satisfy the feminine mind on this team.

Meanwhile, in beautiful Santa Barbara, our daughter Jennifer, a Junior at Westmont College, had decided to go to Swiss *L'Abri* for her second semester. Ann and I had followed the work of Francis Schaeffer and his colleagues closely and thought perhaps if we should experience L'Abri first hand. We didn't have a clue as to how to shape our new study center. In this same period, our colleagues of the *Institute of Christian Studies, International,* had established a study center in Redlands, California and the *Levant Study Center* in Paphos, Cyprus. Now with a *raison d'etre,* we made plans to visit a few centers in April of 1990, and happily touched base with Jennifer for some travel in the process. Thus in the Providence of God, we began an enlightened and sobering epoch in our own pilgrimage.

We are deeply grateful for all who were a part in sending us, and in the delightful hospitality we enjoyed from Christian friends and total strangers – especially at the *Muder und Vater* inns. We savor the memories, but more than that, we must "roast that which we gained in our hunting" that it may be palatable for you, the reader.

The Purpose of the Journey

In order to develop and shape the *Daniel Iverson Center for Christian Studies*, we planned to survey the programs of various types of outstanding study centers such as L'Abri, YWAM, Capernwray Missionary Fellowship (Torchbearers), Greater European Mission et al. From these consultations we would formulate the mission, philosophy, the *ethos* (kind of community), and the logistical, day-by-day operation of the **Daniel Iverson Center for Christian Studies.** We not only needed this for ourselves, but thought it would be good stewardship to report our findings to our colleagues, other centers, and the church at large.

The Procedures for the Survey

Our procedures were quite simple. We wrote the various institutions in advance. Once in Europe, we called a few days ahead to see what was convenient. We had to be content with a day visit to some centers, but when possible, we spent a night or two, enjoying conversation at meals, walks and talks, restaurants, and various meetings in order to sense the *ethos* and *ambience* of the study center or school. We always sought out the key persons regarding the areas of interest, and often failed in some of our survey goals as other discoveries emerged. We wanted to blend in and see the study centers as they were. We found these sorts of folks relaxed but always up and at it.

The Plan for the Survey

The following were areas of inquiry: purpose and mission statement; historical roots and biblical, theological, and philosophical foundations; property and building, accommodations, and community life; accountability, the governing body, means of support, and schedules; the curriculum, teacher and leadership roles; the library, the faculty writings, monographs and the use of audio/visual materials; particular disciplines of work and study, costs, student and teacher make-up; the relation to the local community, relation to other study centers, universities and colleges/ academic credit; special events, conferences, *holidays* (European concept), retreats; emphases – intellectual, spiritual formation, service, evangelism, discipleship, arts and humanities, worldview, etc. We also hoped to make some "Where are they now?" inquiries. This was daunting and daring.

The Marks of a Christian Study Center

There are certain things that stand out about the study centers in general. Their very nature yields the following obvious marks.

1. **The Christian Study Center is *human*.** The nature of the informal community is to be natural. Whatever the purposes and disciplines, one can be and become what he or she *is* to begin with – human. The demand for performance to be "truly spiritual" was not evident either in the *L'Abri* centers or the Capernwray Schools, or in the Greater European Mission seminary in Vienna. Andrew Murray said that all God's ways toward men are human, and he pointed to the Incarnation as the grand proof of that.

The tendency of educational institutions is toward safe uniformity and technique, driven by economic demands. It is thus that God-given personality and creativity may well be destroyed. As Alfred North Whitehead feared regarding even the revered Oxford, the grandest institution may even die under the debris of inert contents that have not entered into the *praxis* of the real world.

2. **The Christian Study Center is *physical*.** The setting of such communities seems to be universally attractive. In most cases, whether a small hotel in Lausanne (YWAM), a chalet in Huemoz, or manor houses in England (L'Abri and Capernwray), these residences were acquired through some default in others' economics and use, and put in the service of Christ. The story of each is marvelous in describing God's Providence and Economy. The buildings lend themselves to the *human* and *humane* endeavor of education.

3. **The Christian Study Center is *economical*.** We found the costs per student ranging from $5 to $15 per day *at that time*. At Dutch *L'Abri*, being in the city, only two meals are taken in the center, and one is eaten out, thus a lower price. Since the support of the staff was through church ministry, the cost was cut to just $5 daily.

We find these type ministries *sacrificial*. These works are never going to be federally or church-funded . . . they are a *faith* undertaking. The Schaeffers, with two children suffering from rheumatic fever and one from polio, had a family meeting to decide their strategy. The question before them was "Shall we promote and use mailings, or rely on God to demonstrate that **He exists?**" What a joy to the heart of God when the family cast themselves on His breast as the Infinite-Personal God.

It is sad that many ministries are mere commercial froth, where the chief end is self-promotion with carnal economic programs. The people attracted are looking for peace and affluence, and will not plumb the depths with Truth. To our knowledge, no study center we have seen or learned about has this problem. Such examples are needed *in Christendom* today.

4. **The Christian Study Center has *unity* and *diversity*.** One Capernwray school had 22 nations and 28 professions represented with 170 students. Although this is not what is considered a "study center," there is much to be learned from these particular schools. Because the costs are not prohibitive, there is more class diversity in the study centers, and there is a transcultural broadening. Today this would be true of centers contiguous to any large American university, such as the Probe Center at the University of Texas. ***The world has come to us!***

5. **The Christian Study Center is a *community*.** From the Greek *koineo* ("communicate") we get *koinonia*, and in the Latin it is *communis* or "common." When people live in a familial way, or in a clan, they have common tasks and mutual responsibilities. The study center is more of an organism as there is an ongoing giving and receiving. Christianly, what Francis Schaeffer called "the final apologetic" may transpire, *with mercy and truth meeting together and righteousness and peace kissing each other.* Jesus prayed that the oneness of believers would demonstrate Who God is and that He sent His Son to be the Savior of the world.

Central to this oneness is intimacy and accountability, which together give healthy growth.

It is in this context that such a center cherishes informal evangelism, which touches lives, sometimes in powerful yet hidden ways. It also is the context for both planned and informal discipleship, something rare in the best of Christian colleges, due to the nature of numbers.

6. **The Christian Study Center is often *therapeutic,* giving *cathartic healing* and holistic *cleansing.*** Some do come to find themselves and God, and to find emotional stability. Some of the brightest and best are different in how they think, and have suffered for it. A loving, informal, yet structured community is the *matrix* for what Schaeffer calls "substantial healing."

7. **The Christian Study Center is educational by its very nature.** Here let us look at the various models which reflect the general philosophy of learning in Christian community, *i.e., intimacy and accountability with Redemption at the foundation and Christ as the focus; of being in the world, though not of it, through both books and experience, in order to develop and adequate Christian worldview,* and act accordingly.

    A. **Scholarship and Research**-Tyndale House, Cambridge, has a magnificent library, and by its location attracts serious scholarship. Such centers where only the most qualified scholars come are essential, and are much like the monasteries termed *stabilitas.* Lectures, discussion and research are in place, and there is a serious sense of purpose as a community of scholars.
    B. **Seminary**-In Vienna, the Greater European Mission Seminary is housed in a grand old historic house of gargantuan proportions, and here students from Easter Europe come for a *classical theological education.* But because it is a small community, they are able to learn by doing in service, discipleship, and evangelism. The theology is seen as relevant and applied.
    C. **Short-Term Studies**- 1) The YWAM Schools and bases range from ten to forty students with prescribed *curriculum* on Bible, theology, counseling, drama, etc. The prerequisites are commitment to evangelism and discipleship. Qualified guest lecturers are used in intensive sessions. The YWAM bases, including the **Mercy**

Ships, are always schools of evangelism and discipleship. Academic credit may be accumulated anywhere in the world and placed on a **University of the Nations** transcript (Kono, Hawaii). 2) The Capernwray (Torchbearer) Schools which we visited in Austria, Germany and England are each unique, but are given to training professionals in a term or two (not over a year) in order to return to their calling as teachers, engineers, doctors, artisans, business people etc. The beginning is often through fun and fellowship called *Holiday* weekends. The converts and those who learn by word of mouth (very little advertising) have produced thousands of godly, articulate Christians throughout the world. The numbers range from 30 to 150 in the various schools. In terms of community, those in the academic terms are in families and groupings in order to have intimacy and accountability.

D. **The Informal Study Center,** such as evolved through L'Abri, allows for students to seek areas of knowledge which interest them – Bible, theology, hermeneutics, worldview, art, history, the church, society, etc. Through table talks, lectures, worship, and tutorials, there is both a community of knowledge in line with the focus of the Center, and one's own specialization. Each person is unique, and this is forever demanding. To see each grow in his own way is love's reward for the mentors.

8. **The Library and Media Center** is often a weak point in study centers, because of both prohibitive cost and limited space, but overall there is adequacy. The L'Abri library includes much audio/visual material and thus great lectures are heard, enabling each a flexible time and way to learn. We see the need to develop a basic bibliography for most study centers of 1200 books and 500-600 CDs and videos. We welcome suggestions of audio lectures and books. It can be built through willed libraries and modern technology at low cost. Publishers and ministries such as L'Abri are generous in this respect. Baldaeus Theological College in Sri Lanka received the Charles C. Cox Library as a gift from the Daniel Iverson Center. The poverty of such a school will discourage you until you see the craftsmanship of glass encased mahogany bookcases, the work of the students. And next you are amazed that they have amassed 10,000 books.

9. **Work, Play, and Study.** We recommend the L'Abri plan for the average small center. Not counting a very few lectures, table talks, tutorials, and "high tea", the student gives 35 hours per week—one-half to study, the other to work and ministry. Naturally, in some places there is more internal ministry as with the old chalets. They need repair. In Miami, there was a balance in ministry and work in teaching English, doing evangelism, cooking, cleaning and maintenance. Our daughter, Jennifer, came back from Swiss *L'Abri* baking great bread, a lingering fragrance of Edith and her recipes, no doubt. There are rather lazy Americans who first do their chores begrudgingly, then gratefully, learning that it is sacramental to work with and for others. The great thing about the study centers and the small schools is that **they play.** There is time for fun, fellowship, sightseeing, restaurants, the theater and simple walks. It is often in such times that the flash of insight comes as Poincare', Einstein and Mozart have told us in their intellectual histories. The latter found that illumination at the billiard table.

10. **Study Centers are *hospitable like an* open book.** One can always find a warm welcome, hot breads and coffee. In Miami it is *cafe con leche y pastelis. L'Abri* means shelter, and as Ann Iverson pointed out, *hospitable* is found between *hospice* and *hospital* in the dictionary.

In summary, at best the study center is a covenant community growing in the love of God in heart, soul, mind and strength. May God raise up more Schaeffers: hospitable, flexible, vulnerable, and available, willing to answer hard questions while living out Truth.

The Shenandoah Presbyterian Church Sunday School, 1935
Imagine a Sunday School that grew to 1200 pupils, sending 150
"grads" into the ministry and the mission field, and was involved,
directly or indirectly, in planting over 200 churches. Shenandoah
was perhaps America's most biblically educated church; where exams
were given quarterly and report cards were sent to homes. Would
you like to learn the secret? To seek is to find!

CPSIA information can be obtained at www.ICGtesting.com
Printed in the USA
BVOW01s0339300514

354840BV00001B/4/P